MOVING?

DON'T LET A MOVING COMPANY TAKE YOU FOR AN EXPENSIVE RIDE.

HENRY P. COSTANTINO

**Third Edition -
Completely Revised**

**TRANSPORTATION PUBLISHING COMPANY
MISSION VIEJO, CALIFORNIA**

TM

MOVING?
DON'T LET A MOVING COMPANY
TAKE YOU FOR AN EXPENSIVE RIDE.

By Henry P. Costantino

Copyright © 1988 by Henry P. Costantino

Copyright © 1989 Henry P. Costantino - First Revised Edition

Copyright © 2009 Henry P. Costantino - Second Revised Edition

Library of Congress Cataloging-in-Publication Data

Costantino, Henry P., 1947 --
    Moving?: don't let a moving company take you for an expensive ride.

1. Storage and moving trade--United States-- Handbooks, manuals, etc.

2. Moving, Household-- United States--Handbooks, manuals, etc.

I. Title. HE5623.C673 1988   648'.9   87-91822

ISBN 978-0-945155-06-5 Revised Edition (2009)

This book is available to businesses and organizations at quantity discounts, when used for sales promotion, business, or educational purposes. For information, contact:

Transportation Publishing Co., Volume Sales Department,
P.O. Box 2309-B, Mission Viejo, CA 92690
E-mail address: henrymovesme@cox.net

Printed in the United States of America

ABOUT THE AUTHOR

You will benefit from the author's many years of experience as a professional moving consultant for some of the largest companies in the United States. Henry is also a former real estate broker/salesman and public school teacher. He has assisted numerous families in relocating their belongings into every state in the country. His expertise in the moving industry, as well as his interest in consumer awareness, led him to propose this money-saving guide to the costly business of relocating.

Over the years, Henry has appeared on numerous consumer-oriented radio talk shows throughout the country, providing helpful tips and "insider information" about the moving and storage industry.

Henry's book has enabled many consumers to avoid moving company rip-offs, while saving lots of hard-earned money. Now, he can show you, too!

PUBLISHER'S GUARANTEE FOR INTERSTATE RELOCATIONS

After reading this book, if you are unable to obtain a discount when using a professional moving company on your relocation to another state, you can receive a refund for the full purchase price of this book.

To receive your refund, just return the book with a copy of your proof-of-purchase and a copy of the final bill (Bill of Lading) received from the moving company, that shows the exact amount paid for your move. By comparing the prices with those in the company rate book, you can easily determine if discounts were given.

IMPORTANT

MOVING? DON'T LET A MOVING COMPANY TAKE YOU FOR AN EXPENSIVE RIDE is designed to provide information in regard to the subject matter covered. It is sold with the understanding that the publisher and author are not engaged in rendering legal, accounting or other professional services. If legal or other expert assistance is required, the services of a competent professional should be sought.

The suggestions given are the opinion of the author only. Every effort has been made to make this book as complete and as accurate as possible. However, there may be mistakes both typographical and in content. All prices and regulations stated herein can vary from company to company, county to county, and day to day. Furthermore, information herein is current only to the date of publishing. Therefore, this information should be used only as a guide.

The purpose of this book is to educate and entertain. The author and publisher shall not accept liability or responsibility to any person or entity with respect to any loss or damage caused directly or indirectly by information contained in this book.

Digital editing by Michelle Fovall
Computer technical support by Elaine Ramunno
Website design by Phillip Ramunno
Edited by Mary Tilton
Cover illustration by Richard Montoya
Text illustrations by Bemie Custodio
Research Assistant - Amir Sadeghi

To Mom and Dad for their incessant support,
encouragement and unconditional love

TABLE OF CONTENTS

SECTION 1
WHAT IS IT ALL ABOUT?
- general background (a deregulated industry)
- determining transportation costs
  (how the professionals do it)
- the "bad news phone call"
  (no longer necessary)
- the estimate, plus 10% rule
  (still in effect today)

SECTION 2
THE NEW GAME IN TOWN!
- no longer a need for surprises
  (getting written guarantees)
- what deregulation of the industry
  means to your pocketbook/wallet

SECTION 3
SELECTING THE "RIGHT COMPANY"
- how to minimize mistakes
  (avoid becoming a "bad news" statistic)
- what Mr. Smart might do
  (learn how an experienced person does it)
- utilizing the process of elimination
  (the selection process)
- the network system of agents
  (don't take anything for granted)

(pianos, organs, cars, boats, motorcycles, spas, etc.)
- extra labor charges
- arranging special services
  (pool tables, grandfather clocks, washers and dryers)
- special considerations for plants and pets
- automobile transporting
- additional transportation costs
- storage (what to do if your new home
  is not ready for occupancy)

THE STRUCTURE OF THIS BOOK

MOVING? DON'T LET A MOVING COMPANY TAKE YOU FOR AN EXPENSIVE RIDE has two distinct parts.

Sections 1 through 6 include most everything you need to know when selecting a professional moving company for an interstate relocation: a brief background about pricing within the industry; how to obtain a binding (guaranteed) estimate; how to select the "right company"; what services are available and what prices to expect; what can and cannot be negotiated; how to negotiate the most reasonable price for services requested; what "extras" are available; how to properly schedule dates for loading and unloading; how weekend loading/unloading overtime charges sometimes can be avoided; how to receive $125 to $150 per day for each day the company is late picking up or delivering your possessions, and much more. Section 4, "What To Expect From The Professionals" is the most vital section in the book.

The second half of this book (Sections 7-12) includes other helpful information, advice and tips to make a professional relocation safe and economical; special circumstances that may develop; how to save money using the Post Office and other alternatives; what to move and what to discard; packing tips for the do-it-yourselfer; what to do if your new home is not ready for occupancy; how you may be able to write off the cost at tax time; how to transport plants, pets and automobiles; helpful tips on organizing the entire procedure; common questions and answers with a host of other useful "golden nuggets of knowledge".

Section 13 explains how the rules are different for a relocation within the same state, as well as local (hourly) moves.

Throughout the book are helpful photos and illustrations to guide you through the entire process. Also, little splashes of humor have been included. In a stressful situation, humor does have some degree of therapeutic, tension-releasing ability. Even for a "veteran mover", anxiety and tension are unavoidable facts of life.

The publisher welcomes comments concerning personal experiences. Comments will be placed in a separate section in the next edition of this book. Therefore, please state whether or not permission is granted to use your name when quoting from comments. The "Comments?" page at the end of this book contains information for sending all correspondence to Transportation Publishing Company.

INTRODUCTION

Deregulation of interstate transportation was instituted to help consumers obtain a variety of new services, at reasonable prices. It certainly has accomplished that goal within the interstate transportation industry. The problem with this industry has been one of consumer awareness. People have simply not been adequately informed as to how they can benefit!

Since Congress deregulated other industries such as banking, air transportation and long distance telephone service, consumers have benefited from the fierce competition for their dollars. The airline industry has been forced to lower prices while absorbing the cost for huge advertisements in newspapers and magazines throughout the country. Costly television and radio commercials also have been used to get the message to the consumer. Banking and long distance telephone service companies have followed a similar course. They increased their advertising budgets significantly, in order to compete for their share of the market.

All three of these deregulated industries have been forced into informing and advising consumers how they can save money, earn more money or receive better service. They are doing a tremendous job of explaining how deregulation has resulted in a variety of new services, as well as lower costs to those who utilize each service. Our free enterprise system has encouraged them to provide this information. Competition has always been a strong motivator!

When was the last time you saw an advertisement on television or in a newspaper, explaining how the consumer has benefited since Congress passed the Motor Carrier Act of 1980? Since that time, millions of people have moved from one state to another. However, few people know how they could have saved money, or can presently save money on interstate relocations, while using the services of a professional moving company. A smaller number of people know the wide range of new and improved services that are available.

Occasionally, an isolated article may appear in a magazine or local newspaper explaining a particular service being offered. Maybe you will find a few helpful tips which were specifically written for the "do-it-yourselfer". Many of the articles and previous books written on this subject have been compiled by individuals who never worked in the industry. They have been professional writers, interior designers, or people with a limited amount of experience who wish to convey their knowledge of the industry. While their intent has been honorable, the information has been somewhat sketchy and incomplete. Many of the facts are peppered with misconceptions that are no longer applicable or relevant in today's marketplace.

Knowledge is the key to a safe, economical and hassle-free relocation. There are numerous ways to approach all of the little details which need to be addressed. The reader will learn how to avoid becoming a "bad news" statistic! By following the step-by-step instructions, the reader can minimize the cost while receiving quality service. It is possible for an informed customer to save a significant amount of money.

The author has heard many "horror stories". Most could have been avoided if people knew what questions to ask, and the variety of alternatives available. If they knew what was reasonable to request, they probably would have achieved better results. Those important and reasonable questions will be thoroughly answered.

The Interstate Commerce Commission was created to regulate interstate trucking. It never encouraged moving companies to use the word "discount". However, it did allow them to "negotiate" under certain conditions. Cost for transportation, boxes and labor for packing of boxes supplied by the company were typical examples. Learning how to negotiate was important in order to get the most cost-effective move.

Because of deregulation, not all companies charged the same amount or offered the same services. Prices and services were similar, but not always the same. There were also many options which differed between companies.

Each company had to receive approval from the I.C.C. for whatever it wished to offer. Usually, if one company decided to provide a new service, most of the other larger companies tried to offer the same service shortly thereafter.

Today, there is a wide range of services to choose from with each company offering its own version. The consumer can no longer assume that all companies are the same. Since 1980, those days are gone!

Throughout the entire book, the author assumes the role of "devil's advocate". This gives the reader an opportunity to learn the secrets of getting a cost-effective relocation from an experienced moving consultant/salesman "inside the industry". Detailed information is included which is up-to-date and easy to read.

SECTION 1
WHAT IS IT ALL ABOUT?

". . . . and the times they are a changing."
-Bob Dylan

Every year, millions of families and individuals move from one state to another. Unfortunately, not all of them move as cheaply as they might. There have been many books and scattered articles written about relocating. However, there is very little information available which reveals the money-saving secrets of moving with a professional company.

Hiring the professionals to perform this grueling task may not be as costly as you think. In fact, it may not cost too much more than doing it yourself. Obviously, it will cost more, but you can narrow the margin considerably, especially since the cost of gasoline alone is so exorbitant.

Consumers can financially benefit from the deregulation of the moving industry which was passed by Congress in 1980. However, they need to learn how to shop for the "right company". They must know what questions to ask, what services are available, and what the alternatives are.

The purpose of this book is not to teach everything there is to know about the moving and storage industry. What will be learned is a step-by-step approach to saving money, while still receiving quality services. Follow the advice and methods closely, from beginning to end. They will save you lots of hard-earned money. If

15

you are fortunate to have your employer paying for the relocation, you can bet the company will be happy you took the time to reduce its corporate expenditures.

In most communities, an educated consumer can usually obtain reduced rates on interstate moves. Competition in this multi-billion dollar industry has been fierce since it has been deregulated. Every company is fighting for your business. You will learn that price differences can sometimes be enormous between companies.

Most people do not know the interstate transportation industry has been deregulated. Most importantly, if they are aware of this fact, they do not know how to benefit, in dollars and cents, as a result.

Before explaining how to save money while getting the price guaranteed, it is important to know how pricing was established prior to deregulation. This segment is not being included to bore you to death. It is essential that you understand the basics! When the time comes to intelligently negotiate with the professionals, you should know almost as much about pricing as the company representative who comes to your residence.

If you moved interstate prior to deregulation, the procedure followed something like this: You called a moving company to ask what it would cost to move to your new home in another state. The company obliged by mailing its literature immediately. A few days later, you received a colorful brochure stressing its safety record and integrity - but not mentioning price. If time allowed, maybe two or three companies were contacted.

After reading the fancy brochures, you followed the instructions to call for more information. It suggested a salesperson visit your home to provide a cost estimate.

A few days later, a representative arrived. He or she toured your home with a clipboard, making notations on an inventory sheet. When the inventory was completed, the estimator determined the total weight of your household goods.

After leafing through a few pages in the I.C.C. tariff book (book of rates), the estimator arrived at an estimate of cost. The "rate" for transportation was listed in dollars and cents for each 100 pounds being transported so many miles.

Before deregulation, a driver performing an interstate move was required to weigh the van before going to the residence. Once the household goods were loaded on the truck, the driver would return to a scale and weigh the truck a second time. The difference in the two weighing procedures would determine the actual total poundage of your household.

EXAMPLE (use only as a guideline, since rates are fictitious)

Miles	1000-1999 Lbs	2000-3999 Lbs	4000-7999 Lbs	8000-11999 Lbs
201-220	$45	$34	$28	$24
221-240	$46	$35	$29	$25
241-260	$47	$36	$30	$26
261-280	$48	$37	$31*	$27*
281-300	$49	$38	$32	$28

Using the fictitious rates in the preceding chart as an example, if there were 4500 pounds of household goods to be moved 265 miles, the rate for each 100 pounds would be $31. Therefore, the basic transportation cost would be $31 x 45 ($1395 total). As you would expect, the transportation rate rises as the amount of miles needed to transport the shipment increases. However, you also will notice the rate for each 100 pounds decreases as the size of the load increases.

To transport an 8,000 pound shipment the same amount of miles as the 4,500 pound household, the rate shown is $27 for each 100 pounds. You should keep in mind that it has never been cheaper to move a larger shipment, only less money for each 100 pounds being moved the same amount of miles. Even though the price for each 100 pounds goes down as the load gets significantly larger, you then must multiply that rate times a larger number. In the example, $27 would be multiplied by 80 for an 8000 pound shipment being moved 265 miles, $27 x 80 = ($2,160 total). The household that weighed 4,500 pounds only costs $1,395 for the basic transportation cost.

This used to be the only way to compute the actual cost for transportation. All moving companies used the same tariff book. Every company that surveyed a residence would have arrived at the same total dollar amount, providing the estimator calculated the same total poundage. If one company figured a lower transportation cost, it was only because a lower poundage figure was estimated by the representative. Nobody knew for sure what the actual cost would be until the entire shipment was already on the truck.

Needless to say, it was not uncommon for an unscrupulous estimator to "low-ball" an estimate. A person would often select the company which gave the lowest cost figure. A "Bad News Phone Call" would often follow after the truck was placed on a scale. The household that was supposed to weigh 4000 pounds and cost $2000 to move, mysteriously became 6000 pounds on moving day. The actual cost became considerably higher. It was the driver's duty to inform you of the actual cost, usually by telephone. Many times there were gross differences between what the representative estimated and the total cost you were expected to pay. You would receive a "Bad News Phone Call" - such as "Mrs. Jones, this is the driver. I've got some bad news for you!" This type of scenario occurred too frequently. Many people were without sufficient funds when the truck arrived at destination.

With this type of situation, the driver would not unload the shipment until he was presented with cash or a certified check for the total amount. If the individual could not obtain the exact amount, the driver would not unload. Crying did not help the situation! The driver would go to a storage facility and place the shipment under "lock and key". In order to get possession, the person eventually had to pay the entire amount. In addition, the person owed the cost for

"What do you mean, it's only $1000 more?"

storage and the cost to move everything into the new home. It was a real "horror story". A long-distance call to the estimator who made the "mistake" would not release you of your financial obligation.

In order to alleviate the hopeless dilemma a number of people got caught up in, the I.C.C. established a rule which protected the consumer from gross miscalculations by the moving company. On all written estimates, it required the total due when the driver arrived, to be no more than the total estimated amount, plus 10%. If the estimator figured the total cost of the move to be $2,000, the driver had to unload if the shipper gave him $2200 (10% more than the total estimated amount).

This was a rule, even if the shipment weighed significantly more, and the actual amount owed was $3,000. On all estimate forms used for interstate moves, a little box was provided for the estimator to write the total figure with the 10% added in. The driver was obligated to relinquish the shipment if that amount was paid upon arrival. The shipper was still obligated to pay the full amount, but had a few weeks to send a check to the company for the additional amount.

Today, the practice of weighing a shipment and paying the total amount based on actual weight, is still a standard method. The estimated amount, plus 10% still applies. A person now has 30 days to send a check for the amount which exceeds the estimate, plus 10%.

What you are about to learn are the alternate routes to take! Why should you pay more than initially estimated, simply because mistakes and miscalculations are made by the moving company?

SECTION 2
THE NEW GAME IN TOWN!

"Now, we can have our cake, and eat it, too."
-John and Patti Neeb, whose last move was 22 years ago

Now, for the good part! Enough time has been devoted to explaining standard procedures for pricing interstate moves. *You can save money by not following the standard methods. Thanks to deregulation, there are alternatives.* Anyone who pays attention and learns the rules of the new game in town, can usually save a tremendous amount of money. In addition, all of the uncertainties previously outlined can be eliminated.

Today, it is possible to know the exact cost of a move, without having the household goods placed on a scale. Forget the unfortunate experience that may have happened to you or an acquaintance prior to deregulation. You can now have the moving company and the representative who does the estimating, pay for their own mistakes or miscalculations. Negative newspaper or magazine articles concerning the moving industry, prior to 1980, can be thrown into the nearest trash can or retained for their antique value. Everything has dramatically changed to benefit the consumer.

Each company has its own set of rules, regulations and services contained in its tariff book. Most companies have similar rules, but since they each apply on an individual basis, not all are exactly the same. Some offer "services" that others do not provide. The Binding estimate is an example. (Most companies exclude shipments to or from Alaska and Hawaii when providing this "service" as well as others.)

21

This type of estimate is simply a written estimate, signed by the representative of a company, stating the exact amount you are expected to pay. A company is not obligated to provide this "service", but most major companies do. They may be entitled to charge a small fee, but most do not!

The significance of a Binding estimate should be obvious. There is no longer a need for a distressed family to pay more than a company originally estimated. Gone are the days when furniture was "held hostage".

The Winds of Deregulation have blown through the moving industry, as well as many others. Today, the tariff rate books are still utilized, but are not always the final word on pricing. Most interstate companies are allowed to negotiate; not a well publicized fact, but still true.

The Binding estimate eliminates all uncertainties related to cost. With that out of the way, one can attend to the other apprehensions and anxieties related to relocating. If you have ever moved, even across the street, you are aware of what those little details can blossom into. The last thing needed to preoccupy your mind is the worry that final costs will be considerably more than your budget can accommodate. Last, but not least, *with this type of estimate a company may offer "discounts" to a customer.* More on this subject will follow in the next sections.

You now have the essential facts of life for the interstate moving industry. First, a company may offer a guaranteed price in the form of a Binding estimate. Secondly, the pricing does not always have to "go by the book". Armed with these facts, you are ready to start the ball rolling.

"My mother said there would be days like this!"

SECTION 3
SELECTING THE "RIGHT COMPANY"

"Let me introduce you to Mr. Smart."
- The Author

There is no ideal or "best" way for anyone to relocate. Situations will vary from one family to another. However, one aspect is basic to all relocations. Everybody must pay large sums of money to accomplish this nerve-racking experience. Even if you decide to do it yourself, it will be very expensive and extremely aggravating. It is always a "no-win situation".

Let's look at what an informed customer might do upon learning an interstate move is on the horizon. First of all, finding the "best" company is always a difficult task, even for seasoned veterans. Realizing this, a smart shopper begins investigating with a simple word-of-mouth survey. Interviews are conducted with friends, family members and neighbors who moved recently. Who has had remarkably good or bad experiences is quickly discovered. If a particular company is consistently recommended, that firm is placed at the top of the list. Using this method, our educated customer hears a few "horror stories" and some tales of praise. Obvious rejects are weeded out. Next, the Yellow Pages from the local area are utilized to find the names, telephone numbers and websites of companies capable of accomplishing an interstate move.

At this point, calls to both the local Chamber of Commerce and the Better Business Bureau are useful in narrowing the list. While membership in either of these organizations does not mean a company is perfect, it does indicate which companies are "reputation-conscious". The Better Business Bureau can be helpful in defining the nature of complaints a company has received from past customers.

Today, the Department of Transportation (D.O.T.) is the federal agency that through two of its divisions, the Surface Transportation Board and the Federal Motor Carrier Safety Administration (FMCSA), govern interstate transportation. If you have problems with your interstate moving company, you can contact the FMCSA to file a complaint or to get general information. You can also find out about various complaints that may have been filed by previous customers of the particular mover you are thinking of using. This can all be done by accessing www.protectyourmove. gov. They can also provide you with the necessary forms to fill out to lodge a complaint or file a claim. You can talk to them at (888) 368-7238.

The FMCSA will also let you know if a particular company is legitimately registered with them to engage in the interstate transportation of household goods. Each interstate mover is assigned a US D.O.T. number by this division of the D.O.T. They can also tell you whether or not a company has the necessary insurance.

If you prefer, you can contact the FMCSA at (202) 366-9805 for licensing information and (202) 385-2423 for insurance information.

Since this agency regulates all interstate trucking, not just household goods, the time one of their employees can devote to your individual problem is very limited. Congress created this agency several years ago. However, it is terribly understaffed to handle the thousands of complaints it receives each year. Presently, it has only five full-time staff members and 75 other workers dispersed throughout the country. This is hardly enough to closely monitor the millions of trucks on the road today.

For this reason, pay close attention to the advice given in this book. You really don't want to deal with complaint forms and claim forms!

After your move, if you feel your interstate mover overcharged you, the other division of the D.O.T., the Surface Transportation Board (866-254-1792) can be of assistance in determining the rates that a company can charge for a particular service. This does not mean they will fight for you should you have a complaint. They will simply advise you as to whether your complaint is justified.

It is important to remember that "people move furniture, and people are only human". This commentary is not included to frighten anyone. It is important to realize that mistakes can be made by the most experienced of professionals in any business. Using professionals will certainly minimize the possibility of damage to your furniture and your body.

By this time, the search focuses on 3 or 4 companies with the best reputation or at least the fewest complaints. A great deal can be learned from a simple phone call to each office. The wise customer notices how the call is handled from the moment the phone is answered. While courteous replies are no guarantee of good service in the future, rude telephone manners often indicate similar behavior later on "down the road".

Mr. Smart then asks a simple question to help determine whether he will consider doing business with the company - "Does your company provide guaranteed prices and/or other types of discounts on interstate relocations?" If the answer is negative, he simply thanks the person and continues the search. *Mr. Smart knows that the Binding estimate can be one of the essential tools needed to get more for his moving dollar.* Assuming the answer is "yes", and most likely it will be, the next question is also important - "Does your company transport *directly* to the area where the household goods will be delivered?" This may seem insignificant, but it is equally critical in the search. Not all companies are permitted to transport into every state. The best company in the world cannot help you, if it is not allowed to deliver into the destination state. The company usually handles this situation by "relaying" the shipment to a state where it is allowed to operate. Mr. Smart knows he wants his things handled as few times as possible. The less handling, the less chance of damage! Therefore, always give top priority to a company authorized to operate *directly* to destination.

The search starts well in advance of the anticipated move (two months, if possible). Even if Mr. Smart previously used the services of a particular company, he knows the importance of using the elimination process. He wants an objective analysis of which company will provide the best services, has the best safety record, and gives the most reasonable price. This takes time!

The search should lead to at least three reputable companies when the process is complete. It will be those companies which come to the residence to discuss their services and give the Binding estimate. (There are a few other types of "discounted estimates" being offered by some companies. Rather than confuse you, the alternatives are explained in a later section. If you have a firm grip on the process involved, the alternatives will be easier to grasp!)

If the answers received on the telephone are satisfactory, Mr. Smart requests that a representative from the company visit his home (at least three different companies).

Remember S.O.A.P.
S = Shop
0 = Organize
A = Ask questions
P = Plan

The representative may be called a sales rep., an estimator or a moving consultant. That person will have three tasks to accomplish. Initially, to discover the needs of Mr. Smart. Secondly, explain how the company can service those needs; and finally, to itemize the cost for those services.

The wise customer tries to schedule all appointments on the same day, or at least within a few days of each other. Enough time is allowed between appointments for each person to do a thorough job (2 hour intervals). The reason is both for convenience, and also to help gain bargaining leverage. If the representatives know that one company has just left and another is on the way, it will become apparent they are dealing with a "serious shopper". This can sometimes produce a lower cost estimate, or at least their "best shot".

This little golden nugget of knowledge is applicable in almost any situation when dealing directly with salespeople. It is valid when purchasing most services. Salespeople usually have some degree of flexibility. Their pricing will often be dictated by the competition. Believe me, this type of strategy does work to get the "best price a salesperson has to offer".

When buying any service, most salesmen will admit that most consumers never receive the salesperson's best price. Consumers are simply not taught to negotiate, as well as salesmen are taught to sell!

Most of the interstate companies are organized in a network of agents. For instance, John Smith Moving and Storage may also be known as Smith-Mayflower. Big Apple Moving and Storage may be called Big Apple-United. They act as agents for the national company. Each agent within the various networks has a different performance record. Some are superior, while others barely attain mediocrity. For this reason, even though estimates are received from some of the most recognized names in the industry, it is still worth talking to people in the community to ascertain the reputation of a particular agency. It will be employees or contractors affiliated with the local agent who may be providing services at origin. This is especially true if packing of boxes is requested.

After using the process of elimination, one can never be 100% sure if the right decision is made. The idea is to educate yourself! Try your hardest to make a wise decision.

Most major companies send fancy brochures to a residence once a "For Sale" sign is erected. All claim to be "the best in the industry", or some facsimile close to that. They each have their own fancy names for various services. The "no other company does it better" statement usually prevails. Each representative who enters a home to provide an estimate will proclaim the same loyal company attitude. Certainly, a salesperson will not come to a residence to sell the "second-rate" service offered by the company. Therefore, try to be as objective as possible in making a final selection. Some companies do provide better services than others. They are not all alike! Listen to all of the facts and benefits, not the sales-hype. *I recommend not basing the final decision on who will be the cheapest. Bad service is never worth one thin dime.* (More on this subject is in sub-section entitled, "The Too Good To Be True Binding Estimate".)

SECTION 4
WHAT TO EXPECT FROM THE PROFESSIONALS

"I know you are willing to give me a 20% discount, but the other company said it is offering a special 30% off sale this month."
- Mr. Smart, when he was negotiating the price with the second company to provide a cost estimate.

Now that you have selected three or four companies to send a salesperson to your home, it is helpful to understand who the representative is, and what he or she does. (By the way, there are many qualified women in the industry today.) They are people who regard their jobs as professionals, and act accordingly. Try to mentally rate the degree of professionalism displayed by each individual. That person is the one you will be dealing with until your belongings leave town. Be inquisitive, and ask how long they have been working with their company.

The initial chore will be to take a room-by-room survey of all items to be moved. Before the representative arrives, discuss the move with all family members. Find out exactly what each person intends to take, and what will be discarded. This will be very helpful to you and the estimator.

Each will bring certain items which are "tools-of-the-trade"; a small "Palm Pilot" to provide an electronic survey or a clipboard with a detailed survey sheet attached (also known as a "cube sheet"), the price estimate sheet, and a large book (Tariff Book). This book contains the published rates for moving any amount of weight/cubic feet, any distance between two or more states. The task will be to calculate the weight and amount of space (cubic feet) of each item to be moved. A total for all items, times the "rate" (in dollars and cents, for each 100 pounds), will be arrived at by the estimator.

Review the inventory with the representative. It will be this inventory the driver will evaluate on the morning your shipment is loaded on the truck. He will take his own inventory at that time and compare the results. If any major discrepancies appear, you may have headaches that only the original Watergate conspirators could describe. He may refuse to load items not listed, especially if any price guarantees were given. In addition, he may call his dispatcher requesting the representative be sent to your home to decipher the inconsistencies. Therefore, be honest and you will not have problems. If there are only a few small items, the movers probably will not get annoyed. To avoid hassles on moving day, make sure the survey is complete and accurate. Simply, it is not worth the trauma!

The representative may ask you to place your signature at the bottom of the survey sheet. Your signature indicates you understand that only the articles listed on the form are to be moved at the estimated price. Never sign the form until you are certain all items are listed. Small things that will conveniently fit in a box need not be individually listed. For those items, the estimator will make an educated guess at the total number of boxes needed. This is a game of averages. There is no way of knowing the size of boxes you might use when packing yourself.

Insist on receiving a legible copy of this survey (cube sheet). This is the only proof you have to determine what will be moved at the price the representative established. It is also used to determine the amount of space needed on the truck.

THE BINDING (GUARANTEED) ESTIMATE

After the survey has been completed, the estimator will prepare a cost estimate for all services requested or needed. It is now time to develop your negotiating skills! Now, you can "have your cake and eat it, too". It is the best of all possible worlds for the consumer. You can obtain a discount, and at the same time have the price "locked-in".

If there is only one or two companies in your area allowed to transport into a particular state, there is a remote possibility you may be charged full price for the move. Also, there is a good chance those companies may not want to give a Binding price. Although this may be allowed, they may not need to do so. They usually follow what the competition is providing. In a small town, competition is not as fierce as in a large metropolitan area. They are aware they have the "market cornered", and are enjoying the financial rewards. If this is happening in your community, PLEASE READ THE GUARANTEE IN THE FRONT OF THIS BOOK, so as not to be disappointed after putting in the effort.

The dollar amount a company will discount depends strictly on how competitive the agents are in your area. It also hinges on how good you are at "negotiating".

Do not be afraid to ask the representatives exactly what percentage has been discounted from the published rates. Most estimators have pressure placed on them to "book the business" at the highest level of profitability. However, they often have flexibility to reduce transportation rates if they feel it is necessary to secure business. It is up to you to let them know of your intentions to get at least three other estimates. You are comparing the cost, as well as the quality of services each company has to offer. Both are of major importance since you will be entrusting all of your worldly possessions with the one selected.

If you presently live in a large metropolitan area with an abundance of companies to choose from, many are already guaranteeing prices for transportation which are less than their tariff book states. Ask to see the rate listed in their books. If you notice they are still using the tariff rate when providing a Binding estimate, inform them of Deregulation. Also, inform the representative you intend to continue entertaining bids from other firms.

Do not get mad at the representatives! Many times, they

simply follow instructions given by a sales manager or owner of the company. They dictate the amount of latitude a salesperson has when negotiating prices. They establish the degree of profitability the company can live with. Some firms provide a representative with more flexibility than others.

In a highly competitive community, many estimators provide discounted prices without the customer having to ask. They are aware of what their competitors are doing. They know what the average discount is in the area. Potential customers merely have to state they are "shopping" for the best price and the best services. Estimators realize if they do not come close in price with other major companies, they are not going to get the business.

Since most estimators get paid on a commission basis, you can believe they want your business. They quickly become equally interested in providing the most reasonable price. It is your job to let them know you want them to "give it their best shot". When the estimating job has been completed, the total cost is of monumental importance, as well as quality service. If you have done your homework, as suggested earlier, only companies with a reputation for providing quality service would have been invited to your residence to begin with.

NEGOTIATING OTHER SERVICES

You may request a company to provide additional services other than transportation. First, find out what services are available and the individual costs for such services. Make certain each service is individually listed on the estimate form, and the separate cost for the service is itemized. Do not accept as estimate with nothing but a series of little squares checked-off opposite an extra service. You have a right to know the individual charge for the service requested. Some hasty estimators may place a total dollar amount on the last line of the form. This makes it very difficult to determine individual costs. You want this information so you can scrutinize these figures with other estimates. Also, if you decide to delete a particular service from the total, you should know exactly how many dollars the estimator will be deducting. *You want everything itemized and each little detail in writing.* Never settle for less. Compare apples with apples!

BOXES AND PACKING LABOR COSTS

Before the representative arrives, decide what you intend to pack, and what you want professionally packed. In order to accurately estimate packing costs, the representative will open closets, cupboards, and china cabinets to survey those items. After the survey, packing costs will be itemized and added to the total. The cost will include:

1. The price for each box (based on size)
2. The cost to pack each box (based on size)

The prices for all boxes are contained in each tariff book, and are the same throughout the country. Packing and unpacking labor charges are also in each tariff book, but these prices can vary slightly from one county to another. If you requested a Binding estimate, you may be able to negotiate a discount on boxes, as well as packing labor costs.

The percentage the representative is willing to reduce these costs depends strictly on the competitive nature of the situation. In principle, it is the same as negotiating the transportation cost.

THE BINDING FORM

After patiently listening to all of the representatives, you will undoubtedly formulate opinions about each company. Also you will probably discover a significant variance in the totals. CONGRATULATIONS! You are half-way home. In order to successfully complete the other half of the journey, devote enough time to analyzing the estimate form.

Discuss all details with the estimator before signing. When you place your signature on this form, you are stating that you are aware the *Binding price is for only those services listed.* Any additional services needed in the future will cost more. You can always add or delete services after signing. This can be accomplished by using a form called an "Addendum". (This is discussed in the following sub-section.) If changes are necessary, notify the representative to prepare this form well in advance of moving day.

THE "ADDENDUM"
(MAKING CHANGES AFTER INVENTORY/ESTIMATE/ ORDER-FOR-SERVICE ARE SIGNED)

When the original inventory was taken, there may have been uncertainty concerning what items would be needed in your new home. Maybe you were trying to sell appliances, sofas, etc. Possibly a garage sale was on the horizon. This is a frequent dilemma. Therefore, as you get close to the actual moving date, call the representative who took the survey and inform him or her of changes in the inventory. Additions may increase the price originally received. At the same time, deletions can sometimes result in a decrease in the total cost.

For this reason, without writing a totally new estimate, the representative can make the necessary minor adjustments on a form known as the "addendum".

If the weight increases, you can usually expect the cost to go up. However, if items were eliminated, ask the representative to reduce the total to reflect the weight reduction (A big exception to this is explained in sub-section entitled the "Break-Point".) Each of you signs the addendum which states the new agreed upon price for the move. *Never sign an addendum that is blank!*

Depending on circumstances, you may want or need to have additional services performed that initially you were either unsure or unaware of. This is very common when you do not already have a residence at destination. A "stair carry", "long distance carry", or small truck to "shuttle" your belongings an excessive distance may be needed. The addendum can also be utilized for these minor changes, without completely rewriting all of the paperwork.

Do not wait until the last minute to make changes, since it usually requires a return visit by the estimator. In addition, the dispatcher (person who assigns the trucks) may need to send a different truck if there are major changes in the size of the load.

THE "ORDER-FOR-SERVICE" FORM

In most instances you should not place your signature on an "order-for-service" until receiving a minimum of three estimates. (One major exception to this is explained in subsection "How Long Is The Price Guaranteed For?") You need ample time to analyze each one, line by line. You may not want to move with the cheapest, especially if you received a negative feeling from the representative.

The salesperson's (estimator/representative) first priority will be to fully convince you that his or her company will provide the best service. If you do not believe that, forget about giving the company your business regardless of price. You can never be assured of a trouble-free move, but you can take precautions to minimize the likelihood of unnecessary problems.

The order form states all of the known details for your relocation: addresses, phone numbers, arranged dates for pickup and delivery, special services, liability coverage, method of payment, etc. Unless you plan to move within a very short period of time (one or two weeks) or have a very small shipment, wait until you know the exact dates you would like scheduled, before signing. Most of the larger companies can usually schedule the loading of an average-sized household with two weeks' notification, going anywhere in the country. Do not get pressured into signing an order-for-service when the estimate is provided. It is unnecessary unless a truck is needed at your door within a few days. It does not benefit you, but in fact, shows you are not following the tactics outlined to negotiate the most reasonable price. You have not done enough "shopping"! This is necessary to get the best service for the least price.

Allow at least three companies an opportunity to explain their services and prices. Whichever representative you ultimately select will be overjoyed to return on another day to complete the order form. Let each one know you are a "tough cookie". In the future, you may even be rewarded by receiving a lower cost estimate from the same company. Believe me, it is happening out there! The "friendly competition" between companies is unbelievable. Your pocketbook/ wallet can benefit if you play the game correctly. Deregulation has given consumers an opportunity to use some strategy. If you follow the game plan, you will get a touch-down and have enough money left over to purchase many hot dogs after the game!

Once you have selected the "right company", have the estimator return. Provide all information which is known at that time. If you must cancel the move for any reason, call the representative immediately. Cancellations and delays are a common occurrence in the moving industry. Therefore, do not be afraid to sign an order-for-service *once you have done your homework.*

THE "BILL OF LADING" (CONTRACT)

The document signed on moving day which legally obligates you and the moving company, is called the "Bill of Lading". *This form is the contract between you and the company.* All details should correspond with information shown on the order- for- service and the estimate. If an addendum was needed, details listed on that form should also be on the Bill of Lading.

Before the driver begins loading, he is required to get this form signed. He will give you a copy. If you do not agree with everything stated, do not sign it. It states what services and liability coverage the company is providing, and prices for those services. It also states the company's responsibilities, as well as your responsibilities to the company. Keep this in a safe place, and have it handy when the shipment is delivered. You may also need this form after delivery if claims need to be settled. Let's hope that is not the case.

THE DRIVER'S INVENTORY

When the driver arrives on moving day, his first chore will be to inventory all items to be moved. He will take his inventory (except on local moves) in case future damage claims are filed. The driver also wants to make sure that what he will be hauling corresponds with the inventory taken by the sales representative.

He will systematically tour your home, placing self-sticking tags on all boxes and items to be loaded. Each numbered line on the inventory sheet should have a description of the item as well as the present condition. Usually, abbreviations are used to denote present condition. He will be looking for scratches, dents, nicks, etc. *You should accompany the person performing the inventory.* Be certain you agree with the abbreviations used to denote present condition. If you disagree with any description, make your own notation on all copies. Write how you would describe the condition on the same line, and then, place your initials beside the notation.

Check to make sure all items receive a tag. The driver will sign all copies of the inventory sheets when the process is completed, and you will be asked to place your signature on each sheet. Do not sign until you are certain all items are listed, and the description of condition is accurate. Review your notes on corresponding lines where you disagree with the description.

You should not feel insulted because some stranger is touring your abode proclaiming a favorite family heirloom from your great-grandmother is nicked, scratched, marred, etc. Most older items usually are. Remember, this person is a professional. He is performing as you would expect a professional providing any service. This part of the job is a time-consuming "pain in the tutu". He is trying to be thorough, and as accurate as humanly possible for his protection and yours. He does not want to be blamed for any damage he did not cause.

Most professional movers take great pride in their performance records and do not like them blemished. Therefore, do not engage in an argument with the driver before he starts loading. Make your notations on the inventory, if necessary. Be patient, and remember he is trying to do a complete professional job, from beginning to end. Don't make life difficult for him.

TABLE OF MEASUREMENTS

NAME OF CARRIER **ABC MOVING CO.**
DATE: 1, 17, 2008
SHIPPER **Phil and Elaine Rummund** PHONE 715-9580   CONSIGNEE same
SHIPMENT MOVING FROM **LOS ANGELES, CA.**   TO   **BUFFALO, N.Y.**

ARTICLE					ARTICLE					ARTICLE			
LIVING ROOM					**BEDROOM**					**PORCH & OUTDOOR**			
Bar, Portable		15			Bed (incl.Sp/Matt)					BBQ Grill, Small			
Bench, Pno/Piano		5			Bed, Waterbed Base	10				BBQ Grill, Large	1	10	10
Bookcase	2	12	40		Bed, Rollaway	20				Chairs, Aluminum		2	
Bookshelves, Sect.	15				Bed, Single/Hollywood	40				Chairs, Metal		3	
Cabinet, Curio	15				Bed, Std/Dbl.	50				Chairs, Wood	2	5	10
Chair, Straight	5				Bed, Queen	60				Gard. Hose & Tools		10	
Chair, Arm	10				Bed, King	70				Glider or Settee		25	
Chair, Rocker	12				Bed, Bunk (Set 2)	70				Ladder, 6' Step		5	
Chair, Occasional	1	15	15		Bookshelves, Sect.	8				Ladder, 8' Metal		8	
Chair, Overstuffed	25				Chair, Boudoir	10				Ladder, Extension		8	
Chest, Cedar	15				Chair, Str/Rocker	5				Lawn Mower, Hand		5	
Clock, Grandfather	30				Chaise Lounge	20				Lawn Mower, Power		15	
Day Bed	30				Chest, Bachelor	12				Lawn Mower, Riding (HP)		35	
Desk, Sm/Winthrop	22				Chest, Cedar	15				Leaf Sweeper		5	
Desk, Secretary	35				Chest, Armoire	30				Outdoor Childs Slide		10	
Fireplace Equip.	5				Desk, Sm/Winthrop	22				Outdoor Child Gym		20	
Footstool	1		2		Dresser/Vanity Bch					Outdoor Dry Racks		5	
Hall Tree Rack	3				Dresser, Vanity	30				Outdoor Swings		20	
Hall Tree, Large	10				Dresser, Single	30				Picnic Table		20	
Lamp, Floor	3				Dresser, Double	40				Picnic Bench		5	
Lamp, Pole	3				Dresser, Triple	50				Roller, Lawn		10	
Magazine Rack	2				Night Table	5				Rug, Large		5	
Music Cabinet	10				Rug, Large or Pad	10				Rug, Small		3	
Piano, Baby Gr/Upr	70				Rug, Small or Pad	3				Sand Box		5	
Piano, Parlor Gr.	80				Wardrobe, Small	30				Spreader		3	
Piano, Spinet/Console	80				Wardrobe, Large	40				Table, Small		1	
Radio, Table	2									Table, Large		4	
Rec. Player, Port	5									Umbrella	1	5	5
Rugs, Lg Roll/Pad	10									Wheelbarrow		8	5
Rugs, Sm. Roll/Pad	3				**NURSERY**								
Sofa, Rattan/Wicker	10				Bathinette	5							
Sofa, Sec., Per Sec.	30				Bed, Youth	30				**MISCELLANEOUS**			
Sofa, Loveseat	2	35	70		Chair, Childs	3				Baby Carriage		4	
Sofa, 3 Cushion	50				Chair, High	8				Barbells	lbs.		
Sofa, Hide, 4 Cush.	50				Chest	12				Basket (Clothes)		5	
Stereo Component	5				Chest, Toy	5				Bicycle		5	
Stereo, Console	35				Crib, Baby	10				Tricycle		2	
Tables, Drop/Occas	12				Table, Childs	5				Bowling Ball/Bag		3	
Tables, Coffee	5				Playpen	15				Card Table		2	
Tables, End	5				Rug, Large or Pad	10				Folding Chairs	4	1	4
Telephone Stand	5				Rug, Small or Pad	2	5	6		Clothes Hamper		5	
TV, Portable	5									Cot, Folding		10	
TV, Table Model	2	10	20		**APPLIANCES**					Desk, Office		30	
TV, Console	25				Air Cond/Window Sm	15				Fan		2	
TV, Combination	30				Air Cond/Window Lg	20				Farm/Plant Stands		3	
TV, Stand	5				Dehumidifier	10				Filing Cab. Crdbd		3	
Trunk	10				Dishwasher	20				Filing Cab. 2 door		20	
					Freezer					Filing Cab. 4 door		40	
					Freezer, 10 or less	30				Footlocker		10	
DINING ROOM					Freezer, 11 to 15	45				Game Table		5	
Bench, Harvest	10				Freezer, 16 or Over	60				Golf Bag	2	3	
Buffet (Base)	30				Range, 30" Wide	15				Heater, Gas/Elec.		5	
Hutch (Top)	20				Range, 36" Wide	15				Metal Shelves		5	
Cabinet, Corner	20				Range, 36" Wide	60				Ping Pong Table		40	
Dining Table	1	30	30		Refrigerator, to 10cu.ft.					Pool Table-Comp.		20	
Dining Chair	6	5	30		Refrigerator, 8cu.ft. or less	30				Pool Table Slate		30	
Server	15				Refrigerator, 7 to 10cu. ft.	45				Power Tool Hand Ea		3	
Tea Cart	10				Refrigerator, 11cu.ft./over	60				Power Tool Stand		5	
Rugs, Pad Large	10				Trash Compactor	15				Sewing Mach., Port.		5	
Rugs, Pad Small	3				Vacuum Cleaner	2	5	10		Sewing Mach., Console		15	
					Washing Machine					Sewing Mach. w/Cabinet		25	
					Dryer	1	25	25		Sled		5	
Total Col. T	15	12	07							Suitcase		3	
					KITCHEN					Table, Utility		5	
					Bkft. Suite, Chairs	4		10		Tackle Box		3	
					Breakfast Table	1	10	10		Tire		3	
					Chair, High					Tire w/Rim		4	
					Ironing Board	1	2	2		Toolchest, Small		5	
					Kitchen Cabinet	20				Toolchest, Medium		8	
					Microwave Oven	5				Toolchest, Large		10	
					Serving Cart	10				Trash Can		5	
					Stool	2				Wagon, Child's		3	
					Table	15				Wastepaper Basket	1	2	2
					Utility Cabinet	10				Work Bench		30	
					Total Col. 2	11		73					

	Cart. Pack	Own Pack	Tot. Cu	Ck	Tot Ck
Dish-Pack					
		3	3		30
Carton 1.5		5	5		8
Carton 3.0		10	10		30
Carton 4.5		10	10		45
Carton 6.0					
Wardrobe	2		2		20
Crib Mett.					
Single Mett.					
Dbl. Matt.					
Qn/Kg. Matt.					
Mirror Ctn.	3		3	(2)	6
Crates					
Total		33			139

W E I G H T A D D I T I V E

Enter item and cube under "Miscellaneous" in addition to completing below:
Boat Linear Ft. ___ x 115 = ___ lbs.
Boat Trlr. Lin. Ft. ___ x 75 = ___ lbs.
Sailboat Lin. Ft. ___ x 125 = ___ lbs.
Other ___ Lin. Ft. ___ x = ___ lbs.
Total Wt. Additive ___

Signing below acknowledges receipt of an estimate of your move based on the Table of Measurements and other information. Only the items listed are included in the cost. Any items or additional services added may result in additional cost.

※
Shipper _Henry Costantino_   1/17/08
Carrier's Representative

	PCS	CUBE
Total This Column	72	47
Total Col. 1	15	207
Total Col. 2	11	73
Total Cartons	33	139
Total	71	466
Wt. Factor (lbs/cu. ft.)	**466 cubic ft.**	
Computed Est. Wt.	**3200 pounds**	
Total Wt Additive		
Total Est. Weight	**3200 pounds**	

Table of Measurements (Survey) – When the estimator tours your home, every item to be placed on the truck will be listed. This survey will be used to determine the amount of space needed on the truck (cubic feet), as well as the total weight.

ESTIMATED CHARGES FOR LEONARD WRATE   **PACKING DATE** 1/17/08

ESTIMATED COST OF SERVICE (Based on tariff 400-e **TRANS. RATE SECTION** 3 **)**

Tariff Item No.	TRANSPORTATION:			
	No. Items _____ cu. ft. _____ @ _____ $ per cu. ft. = _____			$
130	Bulky Article (Describe) _____	Wt. Additive (when applicable) _____ $	Ld/unld-HDLG. CHG. (When Applicable) $	
		Total Estimate Wt. _____	$	

- ☐ Exclusive Use _____ Cu. Ft. Van   ☐ Expedited Service _____ Lbs. / Minimum
- ☐ Space Reservation _____ Cu. Ft.   ☐ Day Certain Loading _____ Min. Wgt.

	Estimated Trans. Chg. 4000# • 2056 miles @ $ $20. Per Cwt.			800.00
	Seasonal Rate Adjustment % _____			
170	Additional Transportation (Origin) SAN DIEGO COUNTY $1.00 cwt			40.00
170	Additional Transportation (Destination) ERIE COUNTY $1.25 cwt			50.00

STORAGE: (Lbs _____)   ORIGIN ☐   DESTINATION ☐

Sec. 9	Transportation In or Out of Warehouse Miles _____ Rt./Cwt. _____			
185	Days in Storage _____ 1st Day Rate _____ Additional Day Rate _____			
185	Warehouse Handling Rt./Cwt. _____			

	VALUATION:			
190	Transportation Portion $/Lb. _____ Valuation $10,000. Rt./$100 = 50			50.00
	8IT Portion (ECL) _____			

ADDITIONAL SERVICES:

115	Extra Pickup Nbr. _____ Address _____		
115	Extra Delivery Nbr. _____ Address _____		
195	Appliance Service (Origin) Nbr. _____ (if third party, enter under misc. charges)		
195	Appliance Service (Destination) Nbr. _____ (if third party, enter under misc. charges)		
135	Piano Less than 38" ☐ Over 38" ☐ Handling Charge		
	Flight Carry No. Flights _____ @ $ _____ 1st. Flight; $ _____ Each Addt'l Flight _____		
	Packing Containers (see detail below) _____		
	Packing Service (see detail below) _____		
	Unpacking Service (see detail below) _____		
120	Extra Labor (Origin) Nbr. Men _____ Hrs. _____ TOTAL MAN HOURS _____ @ $ _____ PER MAN HOUR		
120	Extra Labor (Destination) Nbr. Men _____ Hrs. _____ TOTAL MAN HOURS _____ @ $ _____ PER MAN HOUR		
160	Long Carry Weight _____ Total Distance _____ ft. No. Carriers _____ Rate per Cwt per carry		
160	Flights Weight _____ No. Flts. _____ Rate per Cwt per flt.		
160	Elevator Weight _____ Floor # _____ Rate per Cwt. _____		
	Misc. Charges Itemize _____		

	TOTAL	940.00

COST ESTIMATE ☒ WAS   ☐ WAS NOT   GIVEN TO SHIPPER

☒ TOTAL AMOUNT OF BINDING ESTIMATE $ 940.00
☐ TOTAL NON-BINDING ESTIMATED COST $ _____

ESTIMATED COST OF CONTAINERS AND PACKING AND UNPACKING SERVICES	CONTAINERS			PACKING (Schedule)			UNPACKING (Schedule)		
	Estimated Number	Per Each	TOTAL	Estimated Number	Per Each	TOTAL	Estimated Number	Per Each	TOTAL
		$	$		$	$		$	$
Dish-pack, drum, etc.									
Cartons: Less than 3 cubic feet									
3 cubic feet									
4½ cubic feet									
6 cubic feet									
6½ cubic feet									
Wardrobe Carton									
Crib Mattress Carton									
Mattress Carton (not exceeding 39" x 75")									
Mattress Carton (not exceeding 54" x 75")									
Mattress Carton (exceeding 54" x 75")									
Mattress Carton (exceeding 39" x 80")									
Mattress Cover (plastic or paper)									
Corrugated Containers: Specially designed for mirrors, paintings, glass tops, etc									
Crates. Custom made for mirrors, paintings, glass tops, etc									
	Estimated Container	COSTS $		Estimated Packing	COSTS $		Estimated Unpacking	COSTS $	

AGENCY NAME: ABC Moving Co., SAN DIEGO, CA.   David Sloan

Estimate of Cost - All individual charges should be itemized on the estimate.

ORDER FOR SERVICE

Agent _ABC Moving Co._   City _BUFFALO, NY_   Date _1/10/08_

SHIP GOODS DESCRIBED BELOW FROM   FOR TRANSPORTATION AND DELIVERY TO

Shipper _HAROLD AND SYLVIA SIEGEL_   Consignee _SAME_

c/o _SAME_   c/o _SAME OR HERMAN AND CELIA SIEGE_

Street Address _481 LINWOOD AVE._ Fl. _1st_   Street Address _47 BEACH WAY_ Fl. _1st_

City & State _BUFFALO, NY_ Tel. _503-123-4567_   City & State _LONG BEACH, CA_ Tel. _805-456-8037_

SUBJECT TO THE FOLLOWING CONDITIONS   **TYPE OF SHIPMENT** COD ☒   Nat. Acct. ☒

Agreed Pick-up Date or Period of Time _1/10/08_

Agreed Delivery Date or Period of Time _1/15 – 1/21/08_

Moving subject to guaranteed pickup/delivery program ☐

Penalty for delay $ _____ per day.

BINDING ESTIMATE ☒ YES ☐ NO

THIS BINDING ESTIMATE REPRESENTS THE CHARGES FOR ONLY THOSE SERVICES INDICATED ON THE REVERSE. CHARGES FOR ADDITIONAL SERVICES WILL BE ADDED TO THE TOTAL.

BINDING TOTAL # _5,150.00_

Shipper's Contact Point at _DESTINATION (NEIGHBOR – HERMAN OR CELIA)_ Tel. No. _805-456-9819_

Shipper requests notification of charges Yes ☐ No ☒ Same as above ☐ or

at _____ _BINDING PRICE_

Tel. No. _____

Delivering Carrier: _SMITH MOVING CO._

Destination Agent _XYZ MOVERS_

Location _LONG BEACH, CA_ Tel. No. _805-123-4567_

NON-BINDING ESTIMATE ☐ YES ☒ NO

DRIVER'S PAPERS

☐ General Delivery ☐ Shipper's House ☒ Origin Agent's Office

☐ Other Agent's Office at _____

Date Registered with General Office _____

SEE REVERSE FOR ESTIMATED CHARGES AND DESCRIPTION OF SERVICES

CHARGES AND METHOD OF PAYMENT

Minimum Weight _none_

Minimum Charges _none_

Cubic Feet _500_

Method of Payment _C.O.D._

All charges to be paid in cash, money order (other than personal money order) traveler's check, cashier's check, bank treasurer's check, or certified check, made payable to _____ before property is relinquished by carrier unless otherwise stated. ON EMPLOYER PAID MOVES, SHIPPER IS LIABLE FOR ALL CARRIER CHARGES IF EMPLOYER FAILS TO MAKE PAYMENT AS PROMISED

Invoice to _____

Address _____

City & State _____

Customer No. _____

_C.O.D._

COMMENTS _____

REFER TO THE NUMBER IN ALL COMMUNICATIONS

ORDER FOR SERVICE NO.

_B – 107-60_

The undersigned shipper hereby requests the above named carrier to furnish the transportation facilities and services described in this order, subject to the contract terms and conditions of carrier's household goods bill of lading, which bill of lading will be issued at time carrier takes possession of this shipment, and subject to the tariffs of the carrier in effect on the date transportation services commence.

SERVICE CANNOT BE PERFORMED WITHOUT PROPER SIGNATURE OR WRITTEN AUTHORITY

Henry P. Costantino – Sales Rep. ✱ By _____ This _10_ day of _JANUARY_ _08_

(Signature of Shipper or Authorized Shipper's Agent)

Order-For-Service - Contains all of the important facts pertaining to your move.

ORDER FOR SERVICE
AND
ESTIMATED COST OF SERVICE **ADDENDUM**

ORDER NO A - 503,7 - 7,4,3,   DATE 1/20/08

This will certify and attest that the shipper or a **representative of** the shipper **on the** above noted Order **for** Service, or **Estimate Cost of Service,**
Dated 1/10 - 08 requests that *ABC MOVING Co* make the following changes in the Order for **Service and/or Estimate**
Cost of Service:

		FROM	TO
AGREED PICK-UP DATE OR PERIOD OF **TIME**	1	1/25/08	1/28/08
AGREED DELIVERY DATE OR PERIOD OF **TIME**	2		
TOTAL ESTIMATE COST OF **SERVICE** (BINDING)	3	$2501.00	$2645.00
IF ESTIMATE CHANGED, INDICATE CHANGE IN CUBES, IF APPLICABLE	4		
ADDITIONAL PACKING **ORDERED** AT ORIGIN	5		
ADDITIONAL UNPACKING AT DESTINATION CHANGE IN DESTINATION, CHANGE TO:	6		

STREET
CITY
STATE   PHONE

SHIPPER'S CONTACT AT DEST. CHANGE TO:
STREET   8
CITY
STATE   PHONE

MAXIMUM AMOUNT REQUIRED TO RELINQUISH
POSSESSION OF A C.O.D. SHIPMENT   9

SHIPPER **REQUESTS** NOTIFICATION OF CHARGES AT:
STREET   10
C IN
STATE   PHONE

ABC MOVING Co.
NAME AND LOCATION OF AGENT

Fred Rutabor - Sales Rep.
SIGNATURE OF AGENT'S REPRESENTATIVE

Bernice De Spain
SHIPPER OR SHIPPER'S REPRESENTATIVE

Addendum - States any changes required since the estimate and/or
order-for-service were signed.

| BILL OF LADING NO | 07-5743-1 | COMBINED UNIFORM HOUSEHOLD GOODS BILL OF LADING AND FREIGHT BILL — NON-NEGOTIABLE | ORDER FOR SERVICE NO. DO NOT ALTER | A #1243 |

DATE 1/17/88
ISSUING AGENT ABC Moving Co.

REFER TO THIS NUMBER IN ALL COMMUNICATIONS

RECEIVED, SUBJECT TO CLASSIFICATIONS, TARIFFS, RULES AND REGULATIONS INCLUDING ALL TERMS PRINTED OR STAMPED HEREON OR ON THE REVERSE HEREOF IN EFFECT ON THE DATE OF ISSUE OF THIS BILL OF LADING.

CONNECTING CARRIER — NONE —

SHIPPER JIM AND MARY ALLEN
LOAD FROM C/O —
ADDRESS 25 Casa Ave.
CITY Mission Viejo CNTY Orange STATE CA
TEL 503-123-1235

IN CASE OF NEED CONTACT
NAME Janet Delmonte (her sister)
ADDRESS
CITY Same as Above STATE
TEL

CONSIGNEE Same or Neighbors
(Nick and Nancy Muriella)
DELIVER TO C/O
ADDRESS 456 Naper
CITY Chicago CNTY Cook STATE IL
TEL 803-123-8765
AGREED PICK-UP DATE / PER. OF TIME 1/29/88
ACTUAL PICK-UP DATE
AGREED DELIVERY DATE / PER OF TIME 2/8/88 - 2/12/88
IF GUARANTEED SERVICE, PENALTY PER TARIFF IS $ PER DAY

IF SHIPPER REQUESTS NOTICE OF CHARGES ☐ OR IN EVENT OF DELAY ☒ NOTIFY
NAME Linda Rosseti
ADDRESS
CITY STATE
TEL WORK # - 803-456-1236

ESTIMATED COST $ 3,157.00 BINDING ☒ YES ☐ NO
MAX. AMT. REQUIRED (EST. + 10%)
TO BE PAID ON DELIVERY $
MIN. CHARGE
BILL TO
ADDRESS COD
CITY STATE
CUST. NO.
TARIFF TRANS. RATE SEC OR ITEM NO.

BALANCE DUE IN 30 DAYS
METHOD OF PAYMENT COD

	ORIGINAL	REWEIGH
GROSS		
TARE		
NET		

DRIVER NO.   VEHICLE NO.

CHARGES FOR MATL PACKING & UNPACKING	CONTAINERS				PACKING SCHEDULE ( )				UNPACKING SCHEDULE ( )			
	AGT / DR	QTY	RATE	CHARGE	AGT / DR	QTY	RATE	CHARGE	AGT / DR	QTY	RATE	CHARGE
DRUM-DISHPACK Not Less Than 5 Cu. Ft.												
CARTONS Less than 3 Cu. Ft.												
3 Cu. Ft.												
4½ Cu. Ft.												
6 Cu. Ft.												
6½ Cu. Ft.												
WARDROBE CARTONS Not Less Than 10 Cu. Ft.		none				none				none		
MATTRESS CARTONS Not Ex. 39" x 75"												
MATTRESS CARTONS Not Ex. 54" x 75"												
MATTRESS CARTONS Exceeding 54" x 75"												
CORRUGATED CONT												
CRATES Minimum Size												
CRATES Over Minimum Size												
989 TOTAL					990 TOTAL				991 TOTAL			

	Agency No.	DESCRIPTION	CODE	QUANTITY	RATE	CHARGE		
		TOTAL CONTAINERS PACKING & UNPACKING				→		
		TRANSPORTATION 2100 MILES	001			2539	00	
		ADD. TRANSP - ORIG. Orange Co.	688			150	00	
		ADD. TRANSP. - DEST. Cook Co.	689			300	00	
		ORIGIN TO WAREHOUSE MILES	644					
		WAREHOUSE TO DESTINATION MILES	646					
		STORAGE-IN-TRANSIT	166					
		WAREHOUSE HANDLING	090					
		EXTRA PICKUP(S)	061					
		EXTRA DELIVERY(IES)	062					
		EXTRA LABOR Men Man Hrs	135					
		FLIGHT CHARGE No.	171			28	00	
		EXCESSIVE DISTANCE CARRY Feet	172					
		VALUATION $20,000.	136			100	00	
		PIANO HANDLING	084			50	00	
		APPLIANCE SERVICING	098					
		ADVANCE CHARGE - ACCOUNT OF	060					
					TOTAL	3,157	00	
					PD. TO APPLY			
					BALANCE			

UNLESS THE SHIPPER EXPRESSLY RELEASES THE SHIPMENT TO A VALUE OF 30 CENTS PER POUND PER ARTICLE, THE CARRIER'S MAXIMUM LIABILITY FOR LOSS AND DAMAGE SHALL BE EITHER THE LUMP-SUM VALUE DECLARED BY THE SHIPPER OR AN AMOUNT EQUAL TO $1.25 FOR EACH POUND OF WEIGHT OF THE SHIPMENT WHICHEVER IS GREATER. THE SHIPMENT WILL MOVE SUBJECT TO THE RULES AND CONDITIONS OF THE CARRIER'S TARIFF. SHIPPER HEREBY RELEASES THE ENTIRE SHIPMENT TO A VALUE NOT EXCEEDING
$ 20,000.
(to be completed by person signing below)

NOTICE: THE SHIPPER SIGNING THIS CONTRACT MUST INSERT IN THE SPACE ABOVE IN HIS OWN HANDWRITING, EITHER HIS DECLARATION OF THE ACTUAL VALUE OF THE SHIPMENT, OR THE WORDS "30 CENTS PER POUND PER ARTICLE." OTHERWISE THE SHIPMENT WILL BE DEEMED RELEASED TO A MAXIMUM VALUE EQUAL TO $1.25 TIMES THE WEIGHT OF THE SHIPMENT IN POUNDS.

SHIPPER X Jim Allen
DATE 1/29/08

REPLACEMENT VALUE PROTECTION Minimum value = $3.50 per pound or $18,200, whichever is greater.
☐ Option A - No Deductible
☐ Option B - $300 Deductible

THE SHIPPER SIGNING THIS CONTRACT MUST INSERT IN THE SPACE BELOW, HIS DECLARATION OF THE RELEASED VALUE OF THE SHIPMENT, OTHERWISE, THE SHIPMENT WILL BE DEEMED RELEASED TO A VALUE EQUAL TO $3.50 TIMES THE WEIGHT IN POUNDS OR $18,000, WHICHEVER IS GREATER. SHIPPER HEREBY RELEASES THE ENTIRE SHIPMENT TO A VALUE NOT EXCEEDING

SHIPPER X
DATE

Carrier agrees to transport the goods and effects tendered by the shipper subject to the preceding terms and conditions.

X
Center of Authorized Agent

Leave over ☐ Yes ☐ No

CHARGES TO BE PAID IN CASH, MONEY ORDER (OTHER THAN PERSONAL MONEY ORDER), TRAVELER'S CHECK, CASHIER'S CHECK, MADE PAYABLE TO ABC Moving Co.
BEFORE PROPERTY IS RELINQUISHED BY CARRIER UNLESS OTHERWISE STATED. ON EMPLOYER PAID MOVES, SHIPPER IS LIABLE FOR ALL CARRIER CHARGES IF EMPLOYER FAILS TO MAKE PAYMENT AS PROMISED.

PREPAYMENT $ 3,157.00 RECEIVED BY Nick Shab - DRIVER DATE 1/29/08

BALANCE $ NONE — RECEIVED BY DATE
THE ABOVE DESCRIBED SHIPMENT WAS RECEIVED IN APPARENT GOOD CONDITION EXCEPT AS NOTED ON THE INVENTORY.
CONSIGNEE OR AGENT OF CONSIGNEE Mary Allen DATE DELIVERED 2/10/08
RECEIVED FOR STORAGE IN TRANSIT
AGENCY NAME   WAREHOUSE LOCATION   BY   ON   AGENTS SIGNATURE   DATE

BILL OF LADING

Bill of Lading - This is your contract with the moving company. It is signed on moving day and again upon delivery. Before signing, be sure all details are correct.

HOUSEHOLD GOODS DESCRIPTIVE INVENTORY

CONTRACTOR OR CARRIER: **ACE MOVING**	AGENT: **DELMONTE VAN LINES**	CARRIER'S REFERENCE NO. **G-05-1767**
OWNER'S GRADE OR RATING AND NAME: **DOUGLAS + ELLEN WALKER**		CONTRACT OR GBL. NO. **556-039**
ORIGIN LOADING ADDRESS: **TORINA CIRCLE (#1), MISSION VIEJO, CA**	CITY / STATE	GOVT. SERVICE ORDER NO.
DESTINATION: **BUFFALO, N.Y.**		VAN NUMBER **137**

ITEM NO.	STG CR./ CR REF	ARTICLES	CONDITION AT ORIGIN	ROOM	EXCEPTIONS (IF ANY) AT DESTINATION
101		SOFA	SO - 7,8 M - 6,7,8		
102		LOVE SEAT	T - 4,5		
103		DINING ROOM TABLE			
104		" " CHAIR			
105		" " "			
106		" " "			
107		" " "			
108		" " "			
109		" " "			
110		END TABLE	G-6		
111		PLANT STAND	Z-6		
112		PORTABLE T.V.	SC-10		
113		CONSOLE T.V.			
114		ARM CHAIR	(BLUE) W-10		
115		" "			
116		" "			
117		" "			
118		CARTON	PBO		dented on deliver
119		"	"		
120		"	"		
121		"	"		
122		"	"		
123		"	"		
124		"	"		
125		"	"		
126		BED	(DOUBLE) SC-5,6		
127		DRESSER			
128		"			
129		COAT RACK			
130		BENCH			

IMPORTANT NOTICE ➡

BEFORE SIGNING — CHECK SHIPMENT, COUNT ITEMS AN DESCRIBE LOSS OR DAMAGE IN SPACE ON THE RIGHT ABOVE.

WE HAVE CHECKED ALL THE ITEMS LISTED AND NUMBERED ON THIS PAGE INCLUSIVE AND ACKNOWLEDGE THAT THIS IS A TRUE AND COMPLETE LIST OF THE GOODS TENDERED AND OF THE STATE OF THE GOODS RECEIVED

AT ORIGIN	LOADING HAULER NAME & NUMBER	DATE		AT DESTI-NATION	DELIVERING HAULER NAME & NUMBER	DATE
	(Signature) *Carl Francis*	2/5/08			(Signature) *Carl Francis* -047	2/10/08
	OWNER OR AUTHORIZED AGENT (Signature) *Doug Walker*	2/5/08			OWNER OR AUTHORIZED AGENT (Signature) *Doug Walker*	2/10/08

Driver's Inventory - You will sign these sheets before the truck is loaded and again upon delivery. If you need to make any notations at either end, write them on *all copies.*

The driver will give you a copy of all pages. Keep the inventory and the Bill of Lading in a convenient place. These papers will be needed when the truck arrives at the new residence.

HOW LONG IS THE PRICE GUARANTEED?

Each company providing guaranteed prices has its terms and conditions outlined in its tariff book. Since each one may offer a small variation, ask enough questions of all representatives to determine what is most acceptable to your particular situation.

With many companies, a Binding price can be locked-in for a period of 60 days from the date an order-for-service is signed by you. Some companies start the count-down from the day you sign the Binding estimate form. In either case, having this 60-day "grace period" is extremely important to you. If the transportation rate or cost for other itemized services should increase during that 60-day period, most companies only require you to pay the rates in effect on the day you signed.

When you are receiving a Binding estimate, ask the representatives if their company anticipates (or has already received approval) for a rate increase in the near future. If so, you may want to accelerate your efforts to select and sign up with a particular company, *providing its "company policy" is to not include increases which may go into effect during the 60-day period after you signed up with its guaranteed price program.*

If the person providing the price guarantee is aware of a pending rate increase, he/she may have to adhere to a "company policy" which can differ from other companies. Some will tell their representatives that they must include all approved rate increases into all estimates, even when those rates are not yet in effect, but will be on the day of the move. On the other hand, some have a policy of honoring prices for 60 days from the day you sign up, regardless of what may happen to the rates within that time period. Therefore, ask each representative about present "company policy", and be sure to "shop around".

Call the representative of the company you selected, about two weeks before moving day. Get verification that the "company policy" did not mysteriously change. If it did, and you were not given the courtesy of a telephone call to inform you, consider calling the moving company that was your "second choice". You can cancel an order-for- service without financial penalties. All moving companies are aware that many circumstances can change due to delayed house closings and other legitimate reasons for postponement.

Here is a good example of how you might be able to save money by getting the proper form signed well in advance of your actual moving date. Usually many of the major companies increase transportation rates 10% during the summer months (June 1 through September 30). Let's assume you do not know the exact day you want the truck to load. If you think you may be moving in June or July (after the children are out of school), sign up with the company selected on the last day of May to "lock in" the guaranteed price for 60 days. In this situation, you should not have to pay the 10% seasonal rate increase if the truck is loaded during all of June and most of July (the last day of July will be past the 60-day allowance). If this is a likely time frame for your move, you may only want to entertain bids from companies which have a "company policy" to guarantee prices for 60 days or longer.

This one example can sometimes save hundreds of dollars if a move is being planned immediately after the kids get out of school. The same would apply just prior to any anticipated rate increase, anytime during the year. The importance of pre-planning a relocation and thoroughly following the methods outlined, cannot be stressed enough.

THE "BOTTOM-LINE" DISCOUNTED ESTIMATE

This type of estimate, as well as the "not to exceed" estimate (discussed in the following sub-section), are less frequently used compared to the Binding type. However, they each offer options that can sometimes be the appropriate way to go.

A huge benefit to the Binding estimate is that it can provide

47

an exact price. This certainly allows your mind and bank account to rest comfortably during the entire relocation process. However, a "bottom-line" discounted estimate can *sometimes* result in a lower cost for the same services. The reason is simple. All of the additional charges (except storage related costs and liability coverage in some cases), are usually entitled to the same discount. The Binding estimate may exclude some of the "extras" from discounting. (With all of the options, the percentage of discount depends on the competitive nature of the companies in each community.)

With this type of estimate, the company is not guaranteeing an exact price for the move. What will be guaranteed is the "percentage of discount" applied to the company's tariff rates *for the actual weight and actual services provided* (excluding liability coverage and storage costs).

The truck will be weighed before arriving at the residence, and weighed a second time after loading. *The transportation rate in effect on the day the truck loads is what will be used as the base from which the percentage of discount will be deducted. The rates for other services will also be based on the tariff rates in effect on the day those services are provided.*

The final cost for the move can increase or decrease in accordance with the actual services provided, the exact weight of the household, as well as the number of boxes provided and/or packed by the company. Nothing is guaranteed except the "percentage of discount" that will be applied.

If an itemized estimate contains no additional charges, other than the cost for basic transportation, there is little benefit to receiving a "bottom-line" discounted estimate, compared to the Binding type which is discounted by the same percentage (unless you knew the actual weight of your shipment was going to be less than estimated).

Once the shipment is weighed, the driver will usually call to give notification of the amount due at destination. If the charges are higher than the total stated, you are required to pay up to 10%

over the estimated total before the movers will begin unloading. The balance is due within 30 days.

With this type of estimate, a few circumstances can potentially develop, other than the shipment weighing more, which can result in an increase in cost. First, you must keep your fingers crossed so that no rate increase goes into effect between the time you receive the estimate and the time the truck actually loads. If the rates do increase, you are stuck paying more. (Don't hold your breath waiting for the rates to decrease!) Secondly, if the company changes its discount policy prior to loading, you may also encounter problems.

Remember, while the final cost can sometimes be lower, it can also be higher! For those who do not mind "flipping a coin" or "rolling the dice", this alternative may be preferred.

THE "NOT TO EXCEED" GUARANTEED ESTIMATE

This type of estimate is a combination of both the Binding and "bottom-line" discounted estimates. It is becoming increasingly more popular every day, since it provides an attractive alternative. It provides "peace of mind" in knowing the total charges are guaranteed "not to exceed" the estimated amount. Of course, this is assuming that no additional items are added and no other services are requested or needed after the estimate has been provided.

The estimate will state the "percentage of discount" which will be applied to the *actual* weight and other charges itemized on the estimate (except liability coverage and storage related costs.) *In addition, it will contain a total cost figure that is guaranteed "not to exceed" that amount.* Most companies will guarantee the total price for the same length of time as the Binding type. (Read sub-section "How Long Is The Price Guaranteed For?") Be sure to ask all representatives about their "company policy".

After the "percentage of discount" is applied, the total amount for all itemized services can potentially decrease. For

49

instance, let's assume the total cost for a 5000 pound shipment, after a 20% discount, is guaranteed "not to exceed" $2,000. If the actual weight was only 4000 pounds, the transportation cost for the move would decrease after being calculated at that poundage. If the actual weight turned out to be 6000 pounds, you would not be required to pay more, unless items were added after the estimator took the room-by-room survey.

If you decide to add or delete items or services, make sure the estimator is informed long before moving day. Both the survey sheet and the estimate may need to be adjusted. In some cases, an "addendum" form can be utilized for minor changes.

The "not to exceed" estimate should not be overlooked, just because it is being explained last. It can often be the proper option to select, and should be discussed with each moving company along with the other options.

THE "TOO GOOD TO BE TRUE" BINDING ESTIMATE

The intent of deregulation was to create friendly competition and creativity among moving companies. It was supposed to provide the customer with better services, at reasonable prices. That goal has been reached. However, the industry is gradually becoming a wide-open "price war" where the "survival of the fittest" philosophy prevails.

Many of the experienced estimators have found other professions. The "cut-throat" atmosphere has made it difficult for many to adjust. The veterans are sometimes replaced by new salespeople whose training and expertise leave much to be desired.

Since you should have a feeling of confidence in the person you ultimately select, ask all representatives how many years they have been estimating. This is not to suggest you should disregard an estimate from a "rookie". Many companies have excellent training programs. Simply ask enough questions to ensure what is being promised is both accurate and complete.

Regardless of price, you do not want problems when the movers arrive on moving day. Misunderstandings should be resolved long before then, allowing adequate time to cancel an order-for-service and go with another company.

If you received three estimates for similar services to be performed in the $3,000 range, and one estimator guarantees the same services for $1500, BEWARE! Remember the old adage, "If it sounds too good to be true, it probably is!" An unscrupulous salesperson may call a few days before moving day to apologize for miscalculations or omissions on the estimate. Some may be honest mistakes, others somewhat doubtful. A representative is aware of the difficulty a person will experience trying to switch to another company with last minute notification. Do not let mistakes or misunderstandings happen at the last minute. *If time allows, call the representative a few weeks beforehand to review all details.* Remember, there is nothing obligating you to move with a particular company, until moving day when the Bill of Lading is signed. This is very important to keep in mind, especially if you receive a "bad news phone call" after signing an order-for-service.

If you are searching the Internet for price quotations from various movers, be very cautious and research each one thoroughly. There are some unscrupulous crooks out there posing as professional licensed movers. Be sure to investigate each one so you are not one of the people "taken for that expensive ride".

Most major companies have a website that offers a rough idea of costs involved. Don't rely on its accuracy. When the time is right, have each company come to your home for a thorough price quotation. That's the only way to avoid surprises down the road.

In conclusion, be very cautious of any estimate that seems ridiculously low, compared to others. As a matter of fact, throw it out with yesterday's newspaper!

THE "BREAK-POINT"

(HOW YOU MAY QUALIFY TO HAVE EXTRA ITEMS LOADED WITHOUT ADDITIONAL COST)

Depending on the weight of your shipment, you may be entitled to add items without paying more than originally calculated in a Binding or "not to exceed" type of estimate. (If you received an estimate that allows the total cost to potentially go higher, it would be risky to add additional items.)

Whether or not you qualify, can only be answered by the person who provided the estimate. That person can make changes on all copies of the inventory which will avoid problems on moving day. In order to determine the transportation cost, the representative estimated the total weight of your shipment. After finding the correct mileage, the rate for each 100 pounds was determined. The rate *decreases at higher weight categories* (see example in Section 1 if you are confused). Therefore, if you have a little less weight than the next higher category, it is actually cheaper to figure the transportation cost by using the rate in the next higher category.

For example, if the estimator calculates there are 3800 pounds, the transportation cost will be figured at 4000 pounds. This will be done because it is cheaper. This is where the "break-point" comes into play! Use the following example to learn the basic principle, but *remember the prices are fictitious.*

Example:

MILES	POUNDAGE	BREAK-POINT	POUNDAGE
261-280	2000-3999	(3600)	4000-7999
	$30		$27
	Per 100 lbs		Per 100 lbs

Let's assume the estimator figured your household goods weighed 3700 pounds. The rate for each 100 pounds using this example, would fall into the 2000-3999 pound category. The rate would be $30 for each 100 pounds. Therefore, your basic transportation cost would total $30 X 37 ($1110). The "break-point" is 3600 pounds. If you have between 3600 pounds and 4000 pounds, it is cheaper to calculate the cost at the rate in the 4000 pound category $27 x 40 ($1080). As you can readily observe, the total transportation cost becomes a lesser amount when the total poundage is over the "break-point", and is calculated at the next poundage category.

When the estimator is providing a Binding or "not to exceed" estimate, ask what was figured as the *actual* weight. In this example, you would be able to add an extra 400 pounds to your shipment, since you would be paying for 4000 pounds anyway! Remember the things you were thinking of discarding to minimize the cost? If a "break-point" is involved, you may be entitled to have the representative add certain items to all inventory sheets while not paying a dime more. Remember, it is never cheaper to transport more items, except where a "break-point" is involved. Therefore, start your weeding out process today!

SCHEDULING PICKUP AND DELIVERY

"What do you mean, I can't have everything loaded on Monday and delivered 2,000 miles away on Friday? I have driven that distance in four days, and besides, I thought your company has a fleet of professional drivers?" These comments are usually uttered by individuals who are unaware of the procedure involved when scheduling a long-distance move.

Complaints about moving companies are most frequently heard because of problems with delays. A better understanding of what the driver and the dispatcher must endure, may help to instill more patience and tolerance.

Each shipment is usually scheduled to load and/or unload in conjunction with others. A large van can transport three or more average-sized households. A delay at any of the scheduled pickups or deliveries can cause a "chain reaction" resulting in subsequent delays. For this reason, it is very difficult to arrange a day for

53

loading or unloading, without providing the company with a few alternative days as an option. This is called a "spread". Unless there are extenuating circumstances beyond the company's control, it is obligated to perform the moving service within the agreed upon "spreads".

If you wanted your household goods to load on Wednesday, the company might ask for a "spread" of Wednesday through Friday. This would be considered a three-day "load spread". It doesn't help anyone's digestive tract, but it does provide the moving company with the flexibility needed to schedule other shipments on the same truck.

If a rather large shipment needs to be loaded, the company may agree on the exact weekday selected. (Read sub-section entitled "Weekend Loading/Delivery" if weekend service is needed.) It may also agree to load on an exact day, if the shipment is in a community that has a steady flow of trucks passing through. It is easier to schedule a pickup in a large metropolitan area, since there are normally more trucks available. If the load is in a small town, which is "off the beaten path", the company will need a "load spread" of at least two or three days. If the shipment is small (one or two rooms), even if it is located in a large city, expect as much as a week for a "load spread". It would be very unusual for a company to agree to load a small shipment within a one-or two-day period.

Unless a shipment occupies the entire space on a truck, it will probably be placed with other households. There may already be a few shipments on the truck when it arrives. If not, there will usually be a few others scheduled to load after departing the residence. There are large doors on both sides of most moving vans that allow a shipment to be unloaded without disturbing other shipments loaded afterwards.

Each stop the driver makes as he winds his way down the highway, can often involve a full day of work. He is not always stopping for a sandwich and a cup of coffee. He may have to spend a full day loading or unloading another household. It is a very strenuous, time-consuming, and tiresome procedure. Since nobody wants one's possessions handled by fatigue-stricken movers, reasonable "delivery spreads" are given to every shipment. The length of time for delivery is much more complicated to predetermine than the loading schedule. Obviously, the number of miles the driver must travel is the most important factor. Also, the number of other shipments that must be serviced by the same truck is of equal importance. Poor weather and nasty traffic conditions can also cause scheduling problems. The "delivery spread" will take these factors, as well as others, into consideration.

Scheduling should be thoroughly discussed with each representative. The dates or "spread" should be reasonable, and acceptable to your situation. Make sure they are written on the order form, as well as the Bill of Lading which you must sign on moving day. Do not depend on a verbal promise, since it can potentially create misunderstanding.

When delays occur, your mover is required to notify you by telephone, fax, e-mail, certified mail (return receipt requested), or in person. Therefore, do not have your telephone service disconnected prematurely. When an operating telephone is unavailable at the new residence, the company should be given an alternate number to use for delivering a message (a cell phone number, e-mail address, neighbor, friend, relative, motel, place of employment, etc.). If the company is unable to deliver a message, it can hardly be criticized for not doing so. Always keep the "lines of communication" open.

The moving company may give you an E.T.A. (Estimated Time of Arrival). This is only an educated guess or "target day" within the agreed upon "delivery spread". Don't assume the day is "cast in cement"! Many things can happen between the time the driver departs and the time he is scheduled to deliver.

Today, most major companies have computerized "tracking systems" that use satellite technology to track your shipment 24 hours a day, 7 days a week. Be sure to ask each sales representative about this.

WEEKEND LOADING/DELIVERY

(HOW OVERTIME CHARGES CAN SOMETIMES BE AVOIDED)

It is sometimes possible to have a shipment loaded or delivered on a Saturday or Sunday, without paying an additional cost for overtime labor. If you *specifically request* either day, you are required to pay extra. However, a "spread of days" can often be arranged with a company where the "spread" includes a Saturday or Sunday. If it is more convenient *for the company* to load or deliver on either day due to its scheduling of trucks, you are not obligated to pay extra.

For instance, if you prefer to move on Saturday, the representative may agree to set the "load spread" for Friday *and* Saturday. If the company has a truck to conveniently service your move on Saturday, you should not have to pay overtime labor for loading. In other words, you have given the company *the option of either day*, and it chose Saturday.

While a Friday/Saturday "load spread" option is fairly common, a Sunday/Monday load is not. Besides, it is not recommended to try loading on a Sunday since most offices are closed. The driver usually needs to pick up paperwork from the local agency. Even though he may be in town and anxious to perform the move, he cannot do anything without the necessary paperwork. While some offices may be closed on a Saturday, sometimes the driver can make prior arrangements to pick up the paperwork elsewhere. On a Sunday, it is very difficult to locate anyone.

Other problems can develop when trying to load on a weekend. The driver may need the local agent to provide additional helpers to load the truck. He may also need to obtain boxes from the local warehouse. On weekends, additional helpers and material may not be readily available to properly service a move. Even when the driver makes prior arrangements with the local agent, things can still get "botched up"! Therefore, try to avoid weekends. Do not

Loading and Unloading - Can be performed by using large doors on the side of a moving van. This allows the movers to unload a shipment without moving others that were loaded afterwards.

think the problems discussed could never happen to you. If you are determined to move on a weekend, remember "I told you so"!

THE $125-$150 PER DAY CASH REFUND PROGRAM FOR DELAYS

Wouldn't it be nice if your telephone company, carpet cleaning company, or other service company gave away large sums of money if they arrived late, or didn't show up at all? Well, guess what?? Some of the larger interstate moving companies will give cash reimbursements if they are unable to perform their service during the agreed upon schedule.

These cash refunds are not received by individuals who happen to know someone important working for the company. They are programs that most people can qualify for. However, you must *specifically ask* to be placed on the program. It is not a "benefit" that everyone is automatically entitled to receive.

If a shipment is placed on this program, the shipper is entitled to receive a cash reimbursement for each day the truck is late for pickup and/or delivery. The company must perform within the "spread of days" that was agreed upon. Presently, some companies are giving $125 per day, while others are giving $150 per day. This is money that goes directly to the shipper, after promptly filing a "delay claim" with the company (should be filed within a month after delivery). *Even if an employer is paying for the relocation, you can personally receive this cash reimbursement.*

The agreed upon schedule is stated on both the order- for-service and the Bill of Lading. In addition, both forms should state that the shipment is moving "subject to the guaranteed pickup and delivery program". Companies that provide this program will usually have a small section on each of the two forms that can easily be completed before signing.

Even though the size of the shipment must qualify, it is not difficult to do so. Each company that provides this "benefit" has its own set of requirements. For instance, some companies may require the shipment to weigh at least 3500 pounds, while others may require the weight to be at least 5000 pounds. The time of the year when the move is to take place can sometimes be a factor in these minimum requirements. Some companies have a higher poundage minimum during the summer months, when scheduling is more difficult to arrange. However, even if the minimums needed to qualify are 3,500 or 5,000 pounds, one should keep in mind that the "average" room full of household goods will normally weigh 1,000 to 1,500 pounds. Therefore, it is not too difficult for a two-or three-bedroom household to qualify.

Some companies will not place a shipment on this program if it must be loaded from a storage facility at origin, or is being placed in storage at destination. Also, occasionally there are conditions beyond the company's control. These would include such occurrences as strikes, riots or natural disasters causing impassable road conditions.

When the company representative is providing the cost estimate, ask if it is possible to qualify for the "guaranteed pickup and delivery program". Not all interstate companies provide this "extra benefit", but some of the larger ones do. Ask each representative about any additional conditions the company may have.

LIABILITY COVERAGE

"Valuation protection" is provided on interstate moves to reimburse individuals for loss or damage caused by the mover. Since moving companies are not insurance carriers, and their representatives are not insurance salespeople, they are not normally selling a separate "insurance policy". In the moving industry, it is commonly called "released rate liability protection". There are two options available that range in price from free to a few hundred dollars.

Before entering into any agreement to pay for extra liability protection, carefully review your homeowner's insurance policy. Some policies will cover loss or damage to household goods while being moved, and others will not. Call your insurance agent for a full explanation. If your policy does not presently provide this coverage, ask about the cost for a "temporary rider" that may be available.

It is important to fully understand the extent of liability the moving company will assume. The selection you make *should be filled in and signed by you on the Bill of Lading (your contact with the moving company).* Read it carefully to make sure the "valuation section" is accurate. If any catastrophe should occur, you and the moving company are legally bound by its terms.

THE "BASIC TYPE"
(FREE - BUT WHAT A JOKE!)

At no extra cost, the mover's liability for loss or damage is limited to a maximum of 60 cents per pound per article, for the *actual weight of each lost or damaged article.* This is the basic, limited liability that is free-of-charge but *must be specifically ordered by you.* If this is your choice, you must write, in your own handwriting, in the valuation section on the Bill of Lading, "60 cents per pound per article". This is the bare minimum, provided at no charge, when you are *specifically waiving additional coverage.*

Because this type of coverage is tied to the weight of the item or items lost or damaged *instead of the actual value*, getting fairly reimbursed for any claim is impossible. For example, let's assume your great grandmother's antique clock is appraised at $600, and weighs 10 pounds. If it were totally destroyed beyond recognition, the maximum reimbursement for the clock would be 60 cents x 10 ($6). You can bet your great grandmother would be rolling over in her grave if she heard that one!

In conclusion, even though the "60 cents per pound per article" coverage is free, it does not fairly compensate for loss or damage caused by the moving company. Paying for additional coverage is highly recommended. In fact, it is imperative! Remember that you will be provided with Full Value Replacement (and expected to pay for it), unless you sign the specific statement on the Bill of Lading that states that you want "60 cents per pound per article." This is

"Mrs. Jones, they're the exact same
dishes, just shaped a little differently."

signed by you on the day of loading.

For further information concerning D.O.T. regulations regarding this subject, as well as others, ask the company representative for the D.O.T. publication entitled "Your Rights and Responsibilities When You Move". It is a free pamphlet you should find very informative. Each salesperson is legally required to give you this pamphlet when providing a written estimate.

FULL VALUE REPLACEMENT PROTECTION
(NO DEPRECIATION FIGURED IN)

Let's assume you have come to the conclusion that "60 cents per pound per article" is a real joke. In addition, your household is full of items that cost a lot of money to purchase within the last couple of years. Or, you have collected an abundance of antiques that have not depreciated in value since their purchase. How do you get fairly compensated if damage or loss should occur?

All interstate moving companies now provide an option called Full Value protection. It protects the declared value of the entire household for the cost of repair or replacement, *without any reduction for depreciation.* This is the best protection available through interstate movers. Like most of the other options and services offered, this type of valuation coverage can vary between companies. Some have different minimum amounts that must be declared. One company may insist you declare a total of at least $15,000, while another may require a different minimum. With most companies, you must purchase an amount equal to at least $6 for each pound. For example, if a shipment weighs 10,000 pounds, at least $60,000 total valuation must be declared (10,000 x $6 = $60,000).

The price you pay for this type of coverage will also vary between companies. (Around $10 for each $1,000 of declared value.) For $60,000 worth of coverage, the cost would be 60 x $10 or $600 at that price.

All companies also provide the same coverage with a "deductible". The price with a "deductible" is always less. You

"Honeybuns, I can't remember which side of the bed is *my* side."

can obtain plans with a $500 deductible for $6 for each $1,000 of declared value. In the previous example, the cost for $60,000 worth of full value coverage was $600. If you are willing to absorb the first $500 of the total claim filed, the cost for the coverage would only be $360 (60 x $6). The difference in price is $240. In this case, this is money saved "up-front", providing you do not need to file a large claim. However, even if you did have a large claim, you would only be $240 "behind the 8 ball" since the money saved "up-front" is still in your bank account! The same principle would apply if the total value of your household was very high. They also have the same protection plan with a $250 deductible.

Example:

$ 100,000 of coverage with no deductible

$$(100 \times \$10) = \$1,000$$

$ 100,000 of coverage with $500 deductible

$$(100 \times \$6) = \underline{\$\ \ 600}$$

Saved "up-front" ....$ 400

NOTE: If you itemize your tax deductions, ask your tax advisor about "writing-off" a portion of the deductible amount if you file a claim.

Ask each company about the various options available. The rules, regulations and cost for the full value programs will vary. Educate yourself, so that your ultimate selection will provide "peace of mind".

FILING A CLAIM
(WHEN THINGS GO WRONG)

Unfortunately, damage and/or loss are "facts of life" when household goods are transported. They are simply not manufactured to endure the constant stress of being moved on and off of trucks. If you attempt this task yourself, you may have sawdust to sweep up. If the professionals make a mistake, you have someone to blame and someone to collect money from.

On occasion, if the amount of damage or loss is small (less than $100), the movers may "cough up" the money out of their own pockets. Since they do not like giving money away, they would only consider doing so if it was obvious they were at fault. In general, they do not relish having an abundance of small claims blemish their performance record.

If a claim needs to be filed, the mover's liability will depend on the type of protection you selected and wrote on the Bill of Lading. *It is your responsibility* to obtain the necessary claim forms from the moving company. Unless the company has a toll-free telephone number, call the closest agent for the company that moved you. They usually cooperate with each other when claims occur, but all settlements are usually processed through the company's main headquarters. "Blowing off steam" with the local office is a waste of time.

Most of the major companies have the capability to file a claim on their website. You can do an online claim submission quickly and easily this way.

When communicating with the company's main office, always refer to your "order-for-service" number, which can be found on the upper corner of the Bill of Lading. Today, everything is computerized to provide fast and efficient services. This number is what the company plugs into its computer system.

Sometimes damage can occur while the truck is being loaded. If so, make notations on your copy of the inventory sheet, as well as the mover's copy. This will be important evidence to support your claim in the future. However, do not expect the movers or the company to negotiate a settlement until after the move has been paid for, and you have submitted the necessary claim forms. Remember, the movers will not unload at destination until they are paid, unless other arrangements were previously made. If an employer is paying for the relocation, claims will usually not be processed until the company pays the total amount due.

While waiting for the claim forms to be sent, and during the entire process, nothing should be done with the damaged items. *The company expects an opportunity to respond, and possibly view the damage.* It may want to send a repairman, refinisher or appraiser to the residence for an inspection.

Remember, the moving company is allowed to restore an item to its condition when it was loaded on the truck. It may choose to have this done, instead of reimbursing you.

After making notations on all copies of the inventory sheets describing damage and/or loss, you will be asked to sign each one. You will also be asked to sign the Bill of Lading. In doing so, you are agreeing to accept your shipment in *apparent* good condition, except for damage or loss that has been noted. It is a good idea to write on the Bill of Lading "subject to final inspection of all items for concealed damage or loss". If you should discover that an article was lost or damaged after accepting delivery, you are still entitled to file a claim even though notations were not placed on the inventory sheets. However, your notations *help support your claim.*

D.O.T. regulations allow you to file a claim with a moving company *within 9 months* after accepting delivery. This period allows ample time to discover "concealed" damage. However, promptly filing a claim is highly recommended.

Inspect the boxes containing fragile items and those that appear crushed or dented, as soon as possible. If time allows, you should do so while the movers are still unloading the truck. The longer you wait to discover "concealed" damage, the harder it will be to prove the movers were responsible. If broken items are discovered in boxes, leave them in the same boxes for the company to inspect. Remember, it is your responsibility to furnish "reasonable proof" of the mover's liability.

If the moving company packs a box, it will normally accept responsibility for damage to its contents. If damage is immediately discovered, either the box was mishandled or the contents were packed "improperly".

If you pack the containers yourself, proving the mover's liability for "concealed" damage is always a "gray area". If a box you packed is delivered looking like an accordion, there is a good chance it was improperly placed inside the truck. However, if the exterior of the carton looks perfect, and you did not observe it being dropped or mishandled, it may be hard to prove you packed the box "properly". This "gray area" is frequently a source of controversy. Some companies make it very difficult to collect "concealed" damage claims for boxes they did not pack.

The movers have the right to inspect cartons before assuming responsibility. If they feel any box is not packed properly, they can ask you to repack it. If you refuse to do so, they do not have to load it on the truck unless you write on the inventory sheet "Moving company is not liable for damage to contents of box #___." Remember, they do not want damage anymore than you do.

If you have any flammable, explosive, or pressurized items (aerosol cans, paint, bullets, tank of propane, etc.), do not include them in the shipment. These items are dangerous to put on a truck. Moving vans do not have windows for ventilation, and often get extremely hot inside. Should anything of this nature cause damage, do not expect the moving company to honor your claim. It is not responsible for an act or omission on your part. Also, no company will assume liability for an inherent vice or defect of an article, from acts of God, war-like or hostile action, etc. What it boils down to is, "if you can prove it is their fault, you win; but if you or anyone else is to blame, you lose!"

Moving companies do not allow a shipment of household goods to contain high-valued items such as coin or stamp collections, valuable documents, expensive jewelry, cash, etc. Therefore, items of this nature should be transported separately. You will have a hard time filing a claim for a missing box containing your life's savings or your $20,000 stamp collection.

Winning a claim for other missing items of high value will also be difficult if you do not have some sort of iron-clad evidence.

If a box contains a $500 antique vase, it would be smart to take a photograph and have an appraisal made prior to placing it in a box. A recent purchase receipt would also help to substantiate a future claim. Also, when transporting any item of special value ($100 or more), mark on the box or article *and on the inventory sheets* (driver's copy and your copy), "item # ... valued at..."

Loss and/or damage claims on interstate moves are not resolved by the D.O.T. It does not have the authority to force a settlement. Its function is to enforce rules and regulations. (See Section 3 for a full explanation.) You should contact FMCSA (a division of the D.O.T.) only if you feel the company has not properly responded to your claim; or has violated its contract (obligations stated in the Bill of Lading); or has violated some D.O.T. rules.

When unable to settle your claim with a company, you may file a civil action by going to court. However, it can often be expensive and time consuming. This avenue should only be used as a last resort.

There is another course of action that can be quicker and cheaper than a courtroom. With all interstate companies, as long as both parties agree, your claim can be submitted to an "arbitrator" who works for an independent agency. The "dispute settlement program" acts as a neutral observer. It is an independent, non-governmental organization, which is not directly affiliated with the moving companies.

All interstate movers are required to offer neutral arbitration as a means of resolving consumer loss and/or damage disputes, as well as disputes regarding charges that were billed to you that may or may not have been appropriate. Ask each representative about this. Further information can be found in the free pamphlet "Your Rights and Responsibilities When You Move".

To obtain information about the arbitration program, contact AMSA, the association which sponsors the program:

American Moving & Storage Association
Attn: Dispute Settlement Program
1611 Duke Street
Alexandria, VA 22314-3482
(703) 683-7410

The rules of the program provide that the arbitrator's fee is to be split 50/50 between the customer and the carrier.

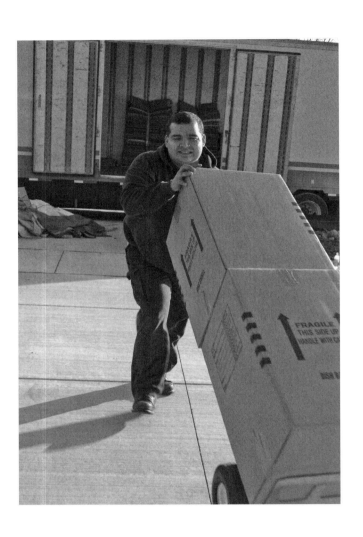

SECTION 5
UNLOADING AT DESTINATION

"Now that I paid to move all this..., where am I going to put it?"
- Eliana, after moving from a three bedroom house to a one bedroom apartment.

When the truck arrives at the new residence, you must pay before the unloading begins (unless previous arrangements were made). Personal checks are rarely accepted by any company. Many people get insulted when they hear this. However, it is simply too easy to "get burned" in the moving industry when people are usually closing bank accounts. It is not good business practice to provide a service to someone who is 1000 miles away, then discover two weeks later the check "bounced like a rubber ball". It is difficult for a company to collect after people are "snug as a bug in a rug" in their new home.

The driver will accept a certified check, money order, travelers checks or cash. I do not recommend paying with cash since you will be traveling with a large sum of money that other people would also like to be traveling with. Don't take the chance of getting "ripped-off". Travelers checks are a pain to use for this purpose, since you are stuck having to place your signature on numerous checks. A certified check is recommended for convenience and safety. As you are closing bank accounts before leaving town, have one drawn for the exact amount of the Binding price. If you received an estimate that could increase in price, have extra cash on hand. If you received one that can potentially decrease, the company should promptly send a refund check to the new address.

71

Most major companies will accept charge cards or credit cards if previous arrangements have been made at least three days prior to loading the truck. Therefore, ask each representative about their usage if this is important to you. For most situations, a certified check is the proper way to go unless you are trying to pump up your frequent flyer miles with a particular airline.

Once you arrive at the new residence, start preparing for the truck's arrival. Vacuum each room before the furniture arrives. Hopefully, you will be able to transport a vacuum cleaner in your automobile. If you do not have room in the car and need to place it on the truck, ask the movers to load it last. When they arrive at destination, it will be one of the first things unloaded when the door opens. If one can be borrowed from a friend, neighbor or relative without having to promise "your first-born child" in return, that would be preferable. You should get this chore out of the way before the truck arrives.

Decide where the larger items will be positioned in each room. Determine the most appropriate placement for the bedroom set, sofa, bookcase, piano, etc. Try to visualize the best direction for the beds to face, and where the dressers will be most conveniently located. Discuss which child will be placed in the larger bedroom, and which child gets the little cubicle. Don't expect the movers to lend their aesthetic criticism or advice. They want to be given instructions *once*! Even the most patient of professional movers will become irate if they must reorganize a room to accommodate your changing whims. For this reason, draw a small sketch with a proposed floor plan for each room. It will help your recollection of what was predetermined collectively by all family members. A plan will lessen the confusion and argumentation which usually develops during this procedure. It may also prevent your throat from getting inflamed!

The following scenario is what you want to avoid while the movers are holding your heavy sofa.

"Honeybuns, I think I like it over here. What do you think?"

72

"Well, dearest Sweet-cheeks, let's try it over in that corner. Then again, maybe it would be more suitable in the family room!"

To avoid this dialogue, put your heads together before the movers arrive. It will minimize the chaos which is inherent when moving into a new environment. Since the driver may need to deliver another shipment 400 miles away on the next day, he will appreciate an organized and efficient unloading process. Time is money to him!

Once the driver is paid, the huge doors on the van will swing open and the unloading operation will commence. You will immediately notice that Mr. and Mrs. Busybody (your new neighbors) will be peeking through their curtains to check out the quality of your furniture. They will be forming their very first impressions. Ignore everything and everybody. Attend to the business of properly unloading your possessions. Take your shoes off and replace them with sneakers.

There are numerous things that need to be done to *properly* unload and place furniture where it belongs. Plan on working with the movers, from beginning to end, so you do not have to move heavy furniture yourself after they depart!

When the movers begin to unload, it is your responsibility to "check-off" the numbers on your inventory sheets. As you are doing so, look at each item for damage that did not previously exist. I recommend at least two people be present during the unloading. One should be outside to check the inventory sheets and the condition of everything being unloaded. The second person should be indoors, instructing the movers regarding the proper placement in each room. *If any damage is observed, make a notation on your copy of the inventory, as well as the driver's copy.* If you notice a box has been crushed or has a corner dented, inspect it immediately. If there is damage to the contents, make a note on your inventory sheet and driver's copy stating "box #__ was received with contents damaged".

After unloading, the driver will expect you to sign his copy

73

of the inventory. In doing so, you are stating you received all items listed, and in the condition noted on the inventory. *Do not sign until you are certain all inventory numbers have been checked-off and proper notations have been placed on all inventory sheets regarding damage you may have noticed.* This is extremely important since these sheets will be used by the claims department of the company should you file a claim in the future.

If you requested unpacking of boxes, direct the movers to those boxes once everything is situated in its proper place. Even though it is not very expensive to have boxes unpacked, *even for free*, I do not recommend having too much done! It is confusing to have everything taken out of boxes at a time when you are not sure what you want placed in certain locations. The usual result is a house that immediately becomes a total mess! Once everything is pulled out of boxes, the contents are usually spread on the floors, counter-tops and tables. You have no idea what a monster this procedure can create, unless you have experienced it.

Do most of the unpacking in the leisurely days and weeks that follow. Don't try to accomplish too much on the day your possessions arrive. There may be a few items you do want unpacked by the movers and added into the price. Mattress and wardrobe boxes, mirrors, lamps and lamp shades are likely candidates. Because mattress and wardrobe boxes are bulky, it is wise to have the movers unpack and cart them away in their truck. If you put them at the curb on garbage day, the garbage collector is certain to scream obscenities if they are not cut and tied in small bundles. You may desire to keep the wardrobe boxes for storage of seasonal clothing. They can be sealed and placed in a garage or attic area with some mothballs inside. They are convenient, especially if you have limited closet space in the residence. You might request the unpacking of lamp bases and shades, as well as mirrors, since there is always an immediate need for these items. Lamps can be returned to their original table tops, and mirrors can be reattached to dressers. *All of this can easily be done by you.*

Do not expect the movers to be nice guys who will take your

"I've got everything under control, honey!"

boxspring and mattress out of a box for free. They will probably reassemble the bedframe and lean the boxspring and mattress against a wall in the proper room. If they must unpack these boxes, they are entitled to a small labor charge for their effort. While the majority of professional movers are nice guys, they don't believe in doing extra work for free. In conclusion, if you want any unpacking performed, have the estimator add the additional cost to the total price. Otherwise, nothing will come out of a box unless your movers are angels, and there doesn't seem to be any angels walking on earth.

When the unpacking is finished and the entire move has been completed, the necessary paperwork must be signed. After signing the inventory sheets and the Bill of Lading, you have essentially given the movers a receipt for your belongings. At that point, they will bid you farewell and ride off into a sunset or blizzard.

TIPPING

Should you give the driver and his helpers a tip, and what should the amount be? Only you can ultimately make this decision. I suggest you treat the situation as though you just finished dinner in a nice restaurant. The amount given to the waitress or waiter is proportional to the quality of service received. I am not suggesting you give a 15-20% tip or any amount that is proportionate to your moving bill. A small sum of money to the driver, and a smaller amount to his helpers is a nice "thank you".

While tipping is always an optional item, by all means reward the person who pampers your possessions at origin, and again upon completion of the move. If you have received good service and courteous treatment, recognize it and reward it!

"Thank you. We'll have to do this again sometime."

SECTION 6
THE EXTRAS

"It seems like I have spent one half of my life making arrangements to put my things into storage facilities, and the other half trying to figure out where to put everything afterwards."

- Rick, a retired marine who needed storage at least ten times for his collection of four wheelbarrows, ten shovels, and numerous other unneeded "collectibles".

You may need services provided which are not included in the transportation cost. Expect extra charges for each service. A company will also charge more if certain conditions related to the move are not within the realm of "ordinary". In addition, there may be extra "handling charges" for items not in a "normal" shipment of household goods. All of the extra costs are outlined in each company's rate book. The prices for some of these "extras" can vary between companies and counties. While the cost is not enormous, you can expect a small amount to be added into the estimate.

Each extra charge should be itemized on the estimate. Any service or "condition" needed at the new residence must be explained to the representative when calculating the total. A few of the major companies do not charge for delivering a shipment up a flight of stairs or elevator. However, most do! Therefore, do not attempt to conceal or avoid discussion of circumstances that may develop at the new residence, simply because you want to avoid paying more money. If everything is not itemized on the estimate and added into the total price, no "extras" will be done unless you sign an "addendum". This form states you will pay the extra costs involved (see sub-section on "Addendums"). Nobody likes surprises, especially a truck driver who arrives at a residence to discover he must deliver household goods to the fourth floor of a building which does not have an elevator. If he must accomplish this task, you can surely expect he wants to be fairly compensated for his extra efforts. Therefore, do not be evasive concerning little details at destination. The last thing you need is irate movers unloading your delicate items.

The "extras" have been divided into three categories: Special Conditions, Special "Handling" Charges, and Extra Services/Labor. While other charges can occur under unusual circumstances, the following is an explanation of the most common ones. *Use all of the prices stated as a guide. Prices will vary between companies, counties, and are subject to change.* The same is true for the regulations which relate to all of the following. Remember, this is only a guideline!

THE THREE SPECIAL CONDITIONS

There are three "conditions" that may exist when moving out of your present residence or into the new home. If any of these exist, expect a small additional charge. All three will be calculated into the total cost, based on the weight of the household goods. Some companies have a small minimum charge. Since some do not charge for stair or elevator carries, be sure to ask questions.

1. The "Stair Carry" (approximately $1.00 for each 100 pounds)

There will be a charge if the movers must use eight steps or more at a residence located on any floor other than the ground floor. Each additional flight is defined as the number of complete floors above or below the first flight. You should not be charged for a "stair carry" inside a single-family home. If furniture (except for a piano, organ or harpsichord) must be removed or placed on any floor of a single-family dwelling, it is considered "normal" and is the exception to the rule.

When the pickup or delivery involves stairs outside any

"Don't worry, just start jumping up and down. If the cable breaks, we
have a 50/50 chance of being in the air when it hits the bottom."

house or building, you will be assessed in a similar fashion:

> 8 to 27 steps = one "stair carry"
> 28 to 47 steps = two
> 48 to 67 steps = three
> 68 to 87 steps = four
> 88 to 107 steps = five

> Each additional 20 steps or fraction thereof equals an additional flight.

2. The "Excessive Distance Carry" (approximately $1.00 for each 100 pounds)

If the driver is unable to safely park the truck within a normal distance of your entrance (within 70 feet), you will be charged an "excessive distance carry". If you live in an apartment building, there will be a distance charge for any travel within the building which exceeds the 70 feet allowed. Each additional 50 feet or fraction thereof, constitutes an additional charge for another "distance carry".

3. The "Elevator Carry" (approximately $1.20 -$1.45 for each 100 pounds)

When loading or delivery involves use of an elevator, you will be charged for an "elevator carry". (The only exception is when the elevator is in a single-family home.) The floor where an apartment or a condominium is located does not make any difference. When inside stairs and an elevator are both available, you should be charged using the least costly method.

If an elevator needs to be utilized, make prior arrangements with the manager of the building. Be certain the elevator will definitely be available on the day of your move.

NOTE: When an automobile is figured in the total weight, the weight of the car should be deducted from the total before any of these "three special conditions" are calculated.

THE SPECIAL "HANDLING" CHARGES

You may have an item to be moved which is not considered part of a "normal" shipment of household goods. If you have any of the following, expect to pay a special "handling" charge. The list contains the most common items.
(The cost figures provided are approximations.)

Automobile $100
Motorcycle $50
Grandfather Clock. $25
Trailers (including utility and pop-up) $55
Tool Sheds, Utility Sheds $90
Playhouses $90
Spa, Hot-Tub, Whirlpool Bath $90
Jacuzzi (more than 100 cu. ft.) $90
Riding Mowers and Tractors
(25 horsepower and above) $150
Riding Mowers and Tractors
(less than 25 horsepower) $50
Snowmobiles and Riding Golf Carts $48
Farm Equipment, Implements
(more than 100 cu. ft.) $150
*Piano, Organ or Harpsichord
(over 38 inches in height) $60
Piano, Organ or Harpsichord
(38 inches or less) $30

*The special "handling" charge for a piano, organ or harpsichord is in addition to a separate charge for a "stair carry" that may be necessary, and not already figured in the estimate.

BULKY ARTICLES

If your shipment includes a "bulky article", expect to pay more for the excessive space occupied on the truck. The following group of items fall into this category. The estimator will measure the item to determine how much poundage should be added to the total weight. This is called a "weight additive". *The poundage is in addition to the actual weight of the article.* (This does not apply to boats, sailboats, skiffs, rowboats or kayaks that are less than 14 feet in length.)

Boats (14 feet and over in length)
2500 pounds total

Sailboats (14 feet and over in length)
2500 pounds total

Canoes, Kayaks, Skiffs, Light Rowboats
(14 feet and over in length)
700 pounds total

Boat Trailers (any length)
1600 pounds total

Travel Campers, Trailers, Mini-Mobile Homes
(other than utility and pop-up trailers)
7000 pounds total

EXTRA SERVICES AND LABOR CHARGES

On a typical relocation, the basic transportation cost includes loading and unloading. The movers should place all furniture and boxes in each room requested. They should also disassemble regular bedframes and reassemble at destination. However, if the movers must perform tasks requiring additional labor at origin or destination, expect a small additional charge. The labor rates vary from county to county.

Some examples would be outdoor swing sets or storage sheds that need disassembling and/or reassembling. Discuss the cost with the estimator when the total is being calculated. These items should be dismantled and can easily be done with "a little help from

"I don't know if we still have room for the vacuum cleaner!"

a friend". Do not assume the movers will perform these extra tasks unless they are paid for their labor.

If you *specifically request* labor performed between 5:00 p.m. and 8:00 a.m., overtime labor rates will apply. This is also true if you *specifically request* labor performed on Saturdays, Sundays or Holidays. Therefore, try to avoid these circumstances.

EXTRA PICKUP OR DELIVERY

There may be large items which need to be included in a shipment, but are not at the residence. Small things do not present a problem, since they can usually be transported in an automobile. However, what does one do when Aunt Lucy's antique piano is sitting in her garage 10 blocks away? Or, what about the bedroom set received as a wedding gift, but the furniture store is asking $100 to deliver? Or, there is the public storage unit that was rented to stuff all those unneeded things that would not fit into your present residence.

The truck that is scheduled to come to your house can also make a stop before or after loading at your residence. This would need to be arranged and calculated into the total cost. Discuss your situation when the representative provides the estimate. While it is not very expensive (approximately $50 for each stop), the mileage between stops will be added to the total miles. If that total makes it necessary to calculate in a higher mileage category, the result will be a slightly higher transportation cost. Ask the representative if the distance between your residence and the extra stop will affect the "rate". If it does increase, the amount should be small.

If you decide to have the moving company perform any extra stops, find out what mileage limitations they may have. There is a limit to the number of miles the movers will travel to accomplish this extra service. If it is a reasonable distance or "en route", there should be no problem. However, if you are moving from Los Angeles to New York City and have an extra pickup in Oregon, you can obviously forget it!

"THIRD PARTY" SERVICES

This type of service is needed for items requiring special treatment at origin and/or destination. *It is a special service provided by a different company.* The moving company can be a good source of information to locate qualified people to perform these services. It can usually make the necessary arrangements for you, but will probably add a small charge to do so. Get the name of qualified people to call, and save the cost of whatever commission the moving company may tack on. Besides, most moving companies do not like to get involved in this separate billing procedure.

Washer/Dryer - In order to transport a washer, the water hoses must be disconnected. There is also a styrofoam "washer block" available to place inside the machine to keep the agitator secured. These blocks can be purchased from most moving companies.

If you do not want to disconnect the water hoses and/or reconnect at destination, the moving company can make arrangements for a "third party" company to perform this easy task. If you want to make your own arrangements, just get the name of a "specialist" within the area. The same appliance specialist can also service a gas dryer which needs to be disconnected from the gas outlet.

Washer and dryer disconnections are not difficult. Each can easily be done with a pair of pliers. The local hardware store will have a small metal cap to screw on the gas outlet protruding from the wall.

Most movers do not want to perform this work because of a potential liability problem. If the water faucets are not closed properly or are defective, the water damage could be costly. If the gas shut-off valve is not closed properly and a leak develops, an explosion could occur. The movers do not want to accept responsibility for either situation. The probability of a problem occurring is small. However, legal problems have occurred in the past to discourage movers from being overly accommodating in this department. Their insurance rates are excessive because of the high risk nature of the business. The last thing they need is to have their coverage quadrupled or even dropped as a result of a major claim due to disconnecting a washer or dryer.

Pool Tables - If you have a small pool table, you can probably get by with taking the legs off. If you need to move a full-sized table with large pieces of slate, special servicing is usually required. The table should be disassembled with the slate placed in wooden crates. Your mover should be able to provide the name of a specialty company to do this. Companies that sell pool tables can also provide this information. When the time comes for reassembly in your new home, the Yellow Pages can be used to locate another company. A better idea would be to call the local agency of the company that moved you. It can provide valuable information. Ask for recommendations for whatever services are required. This will take the guesswork out of selecting a reputable company with reasonable prices.

Grandfather Clocks - If you have a grandfather clock with a pendulum and weights, they need to be placed in a box. If the clock has a complicated timing mechanism, a clock specialist should be used to disassemble and reassemble at destination. If the outer part of your clock is antique or somewhat fragile, the moving company can construct a wooden crate. Ask the estimator to measure and calculate the cost into the estimate.

The movers will construct and place the clock in a wooden crate, but they don't like to get involved in disassembly of the timing mechanism. These are precision items that should be handled by a specialist. They are specialists in moving! Do not expect them to be "jacks of all trades". Besides, some of them have hands that would never fit into Aunt Gertrude's antique clock!

TRANSPORTING PLANTS

Placing potted plants in the same van with household goods can be expensive. When you are paying for transportation on a poundage basis, dirt is expensive to move since it can be very heavy. One potted plant can sometimes weigh 50 pounds or more. When you consider the cost for each 100 pounds being moved, it is often

"Mrs. Jones, I may need your assistance!"

cheaper and less risky to buy healthy ones later on.

Even if you are willing to pay to transport plants that have been "members of the family" for 10 years, no company will guarantee their survival. You may be doing those "prized possessions" a big favor by finding another happy home where they can flourish. Also, if you sell the "babies", that revenue can be used to purchase a new family at the other end. Bidding farewell to loved ones is always a difficult task.

Some states have restrictions that prohibit certain types of plants from entering. Others will allow entry if they have been already certified by state or federal pest control officials. You will have to call or write to the appropriate agricultural agency for the state you are moving into. Many states have brochures to send in response to inquiries. Before making a long-distance call, first try the local office of the State Department of Agriculture.

The prohibition is enforced to prevent nasty little bugs from infesting or contaminating the land. A few states are so concerned that they do not allow any plants to enter. Some allow certain plants, only if proof is available to show they have been properly sprayed.

If you are still reading about how to transport your plants, one might assume that you have not been totally discouraged yet. However, there is one more "whammo" involved in the process. *The movers cannot be forced to load them on the truck.* It is sort of the "driver's discretion". *If he feels your plants may infest his van, he has the right to refuse to load them.* He does not want bugs in his truck, anymore than you want them in your new home.

In conclusion, if you are willing to pay the price; endure the bureaucratic red tape; and take a gamble on the driver; your loyalty and persistence should be commended. However, the results of the "ultimate gamble" will not be known until your plants finally arrive at destination, alive.

If you are able to place a few of your most "loyal buddies" in the car, never put them in the trunk. Any extreme temperature changes can be disastrous. Water them a day before leaving and securely place in a cardboard box. Use newspaper to prevent the pots from moving, and be sure to line the box with a plastic trashbag beforehand. You do not want water seepage to ruin the cardboard and car seat. Do not over-water the plants before leaving, since you can always find water at "pit-stops".

Once your plants reach destination, place them in an environment they are accustomed to. Try to duplicate the same amount of light and shade which nurtured them in the past.

TRANSPORTING PETS

Since the movers will not place "Fee-Fee" in the truck, special arrangements will need to be made. The moving company should be able to provide the name of a "pet transportation" company if you do not want to take "Fee-Fee" with you. No matter what method is chosen, be sure to discuss with your veterinarian, any special requirements and precautions that must be considered. Many states require interstate health certificates and entry permits.

Requirements vary from one state to another. Most require rabies immunization and licensing for dogs. Some states also require that cats be licensed. Your local humane society or kennel can be a good source of information. If the veterinarian has a medical file for your pet, you may want to have that information forwarded to a veterinarian in your new community. Ask for a referral or recommendation.

When traveling by automobile, use a pet carrier or crate in the back seat. You do not need "Fee-Fee" jumping around, disturbing your concentration. To help your pet adjust before the trip, place the food and water bowl inside the container with the door constantly open. Give your pet ample time to adjust to the temporary quarters. To help it get accustomed to automobile transportation, a few short rides before the trip will be helpful.

While traveling, exercise your pet at the reststops. Always place a leash on the collar when doing so. New surroundings, curiosity, and normal nervousness can cause it to scamper away. You do not need unnecessary delays. If you must leave your pet in the car, avoid parking in the hot sun and be sure to leave the windows open a few inches.

Some airlines will transport pets if certain requirements are met. Size and construction of the container is important. They will not be overjoyed to see "Fee-Fee's" huge doghouse on the conveyor belt. Since most airlines limit baggage department space for pet transportation, make a reservation early. Also, during winter months, airlines will not place pets in unheated baggage areas.

No matter what method is used for transportation, sedation is sometimes required. Always consult a veterinarian before tranquilizing any pet.

TRANSPORTING AUTOMOBILES

If you are not overjoyed with the idea of driving your car on a long trip, there are a few options available to ease the burden. It is not a cheap service to arrange, but it can be a convenient luxury for those willing to pay the price.

One convenient method is to have the car loaded on the same truck with the household goods. Car ramps are utilized for this procedure. Once the vehicle is in position, tension straps are used to firmly hold down the suspension system. A platform is usually constructed over the car enabling the space above to be used for household goods.

It is not safe to place any items in the area surrounding the car. Also, it is not safe to pack the inside of the car with items that can be jostled around every time the truck drives over a bump. Car seats can quickly transform into trampolines. This method is very convenient since everything can usually be loaded and delivered in one day at each end.

Another method which can often be less expensive is by using a "car carrier" truck. This is the type of vehicle used by car

Car Carrier - Vehicle used exclusively
for automobile transportation.

manufacturers when delivering new cars to a dealership. Many of the larger companies that transport household goods also have a fleet of "car carriers". While it is sometimes less expensive than placing a car on a moving van, you can usually expect a little inconvenience. There is a good chance the "car carrier" and the moving van will not load and/or deliver on the same day. Each vehicle will probably have a different schedule. If you don't mind waiting a few days for your car to arrive, the "car carrier" may be preferred. If you do not have an immediate need for the vehicle prior to departure, it is definitely worth considering. This is especially true if you must rent a car at your new location. However, since the "car carrier" may arrive at destination before you (if you are driving another vehicle), you may need to make arrangements for someone else to accept delivery and pay the driver. If you have more than one car to transport, the "car carrier" method is highly recommended. You will pay a fixed price (depending on mileage) for the first car. The cost for each additional car goes down when loaded as one shipment. The weight of a car is irrelevant when the "car carrier" method is used.

There are companies that specialize in automobile transportation (some even use railroad cars), and never handle household goods. If you are considering the use of a "car carrier", you can probably save money by making separate arrangements. They are usually cheaper than a company which specializes in household goods transportation. The names of these companies can be found in the Yellow Pages, on the Internet, or in the classified section of your newspaper.

After learning how much it will cost to transport your car, you may feel it is too expensive. There is an inexpensive alternative which can be used, but there is some risk involved. "Auto Drive-Away" agencies are located throughout the country which make arrangements to have people (often college students) drive the car for you. The problem is that you never know the driving record of the individual you have entrusted with the car. If you are willing to pay a few hundred dollars, and take the gamble, this option may be for you. These companies are listed in the Yellow Pages under "Auto Transporters", or in the classified section of the newspaper.

Another method would be to tow one car behind another you are driving. However, since a car can easily weigh over 2500 pounds, you had better be sure the vehicle that must pull the weight, is capable of doing so. Pulling over a ton of metal, especially up mountains, can be a strain on most car engines. Consult with a mechanic before making a decision. If this is the method selected, "tow bars" and "tow dollies" (for cars that will not fit on a "tow bar") can be rented from most truck rental agencies.

ADDITIONAL TRANSPORTATION COSTS

You may notice an extra charge for something which you never requested. A small charge may be listed under "additional transportation cost". They are based on the cost of doing business (cost of labor) in each county. It is sort of a "labor equalization factor". Rates can vary from zero to a few dollars for each 100 pounds.

There is a good reason for listing these rates separately. When loading or unloading a shipment, the driver often needs to request extra labor from a local agent. He may or may not have a partner who travels with him from one location to the next. Even if he does, he often needs a third or fourth person to help with loading or unloading.

The basic transportation rate does not incorporate all expenses incurred by the driver, in all circumstances. Therefore, the "additional transportation cost" is used to compensate the driver for the additional expense he may have when "doing business" in an expensive county.

FUEL SURCHARGE

Every person reading this book is aware of the cost of gasoline today (2008). The cost of fuel to transport household goods is "going through the roof". For this reason, as the gasoline cost fluctuates, the "fuel surcharge" will also. The exact percentage should be itemized and is a percentage of the cost to transport only, not the total bill. This percentage will vary between companies.

STORAGE
(WHEN THE NEW HOME IS NOT READY)

If your new residence is not immediately available for occupancy, warehouse storage may be needed at origin or destination. The rate for each 100 pounds for storage-in-transit (S.I.T.) can vary between companies and counties. Since one county can be cheaper than another, ask each representative for the rates in your present location, as well as the destination county. There can be a huge price difference. (All costs related to S.I.T. are usually not discounted.)

The moving company is allowed to hold a shipment in S.I.T for up to 90 days. The rates are usually not guaranteed, but even if an increase should occur while your goods are in storage, it probably would not be excessive.

Individual rates per 100 pounds are calculated for: the first day in warehouse, each additional day (up to 90 days in total), warehouse handling, and pickup or delivery labor. In addition, a small charge will be assessed for valuation coverage for each month in storage (unless you specifically waive this).

After the S.I.T. period exceeds 90 days, the interstate nature of the shipment terminates. All costs will usually change since they become subject to the rates, terms, and conditions of the local warehouse. Charges for storage, as well as all labor costs, will no longer have to be based on poundage. The entire shipment will convert to "permanent storage" status and a separate contract with the local warehouse will be needed. When the conversion takes place, the prices will sometimes be more, sometimes stay the same, and often they will decrease. It will depend on the "cost of doing business" in that particular community.

When trying to decide whether to have your possessions stored at origin or destination, another factor in addition to cost, needs to be considered. Individual circumstances determine what will be *most convenient*. If you are sure that you will need to remove items from the warehouse, you will want everything stored where

you plan on being. Regardless of cost, you may have no choice. If removal of items is necessary, you can expect to pay an "access charge" for someone in the warehouse to help find what you need to remove. This is done on an hourly basis.

Removal of items can be a costly proposition. When your shipment arrives, it will probably be placed into large plywood containers. They are called "pallets" or "vaults". A forklift is used to move and stack these containers once they are sealed shut. Trying to figure out which container has the items you need to remove is like trying to find a "needle in a haystack". This is why the hourly "access charge" can add up.

If all of the related costs are similar at both origin and destination, and there are no extenuating circumstances, it is wise to have your shipment stored at destination. Once you are ready for final delivery, local arrangements can be made quickly and easily. A local phone call or visit to the nearby warehouse will certainly be more convenient.

If you are contemplating having your shipment delivered to a "public storage" facility, certain considerations need to be addressed. You will need to *carefully inspect everything for damage and/or loss* during the unloading process. Even though you are allowed 9 months after delivery to file a claim, if you make separate arrangements to move everything from a public storage facility, the company that delivered the shipment will undoubtedly fight a future claim. If you didn't make notations on the driver's inventory sheets at origin or at delivery, the company will probably take the position that the damage or loss occurred after it relinquished the shipment.

The biggest benefit in using a public storage facility is your ability to remove items at no extra cost. In addition, there is no warehouse labor cost to place everything into "pallets", and sometimes the monthly storage cost can be lower.

When selecting a conveniently located self-storage facility, it is very important to ask the manager if large moving vans are allowed to enter. Very often, they are not allowed in. This is due to the fact that large trucks simply cannot make the turns necessary to get in or out of the facility. If you still want to place your shipment there, be expecting the movers to charge extra to park their truck on the street in order to "shuttle" your belongings into your unit.

Since the movers will be taking their furniture pads with them, you will need plenty of blankets or padding. Ask the manager of the storage facility where they can be rented on a monthly basis. You will need to adequately protect all items being placed in the cubicle, and when loading a truck in the future. Do not be skimpy in this department.

Storage Vaults - A forklift is used to stack wooden vaults inside the warehouse.

Typical self-storage facility. It's extremely important to inquire before delivery as to whether large moving vans are allowed on property.

SECTION 7
PACKING

"If I need to move one more time, all I will need is a little wagon."
  - Steve, a retired air force colonel who has "weeded out" his possessions 15 times in the past 20 years.

WHAT TO KEEP AND WHAT TO DUMP

A popular misconception is that it's cheaper to send a larger shipment. While it is correct to assume that the rate (amount of dollars for each 100 pounds) decreases as the size of a shipment significantly increases, you must keep in mind that the "multiplier" increases. So, before you start thinking about whether you or the moving company will perform the grueling task of packing, the entire family should engage in a "sort and weed" routine. The goal is to lighten the load as much as possible. Family members should objectively decide what they *really* will have a need or use for at destination. The borderline items should be part of a group discussion.

Everyone has sentimental or "maybe-some-day" STUFF. The daughter in high school has "Jake", the wooden horse she rode while in kindergarten; the mother has 10 cast iron skillets, but only uses her favorite one for cooking each day; the father has two walnut antique dressers that he was supposed to refinish 15 years ago; the son has every pair of shoes and sneakers worn since grammar school and he is now in medical school; and the list of STUFF goes on and on!

Designate an area in the garage, basement or attic where

"This is easy, but what do I do with the goldfish?"

everyone can slowly place the "dumpers". When the process is complete, plan a garage sale. When it is over, invite relatives, neighbors or friends to stop by and select what they need. In doing so, you will leave the community with a lot of happy faces bidding farewell. Lastly, call a charitable organization such as the Salvation Army or Goodwill Industries. They will usually send a truck to pick up the remaining items. However, sometimes you may be stuck bringing everything to them. In either case, make sure you get a receipt. You may be able to qualify for a charitable tax deduction on an itemized income tax return with the IRS.

Even though a few decisions will be made on a sentimental and personal basis, many can be logical and practical. Let's explore some typical considerations.

Alcoholic Beverages. They are illegal to include in an interstate shipment of household goods.

Appliances. Washers, dryers, stoves, dishwashers, refrigerators, and freezers are typically the most expensive items to move. Each one can sometimes cost $100-$200 to relocate. If any of these appliances are old or not performing like they used to, they are likely candidates to sell. Placing a "Classified" advertisement in the local newspaper may be the answer. If you are selling or renting your residence, maybe the purchaser or future tenant would be interested.

Even if an appliance is relatively new, you must decide whether or not you have a need for it in your new home. Many houses, apartments and condominiums contain built-in stoves, dishwashers and trash compactors. In addition, some homes are "all electric". A gas stove or dryer will not easily plug into an electrical outlet. It would be a shame to needlessly pay for moving these items. Also, the size and, or color of the appliance may not be appropriate with the new decor. In some cases, it is wise to use the money from selling an appliance, *plus the money saved by not moving it,* toward the purchase of a new one at the other end.

Books. (Read section called "Using the Post Office".)

Clothing. For clothing which is presently hanging in a closet, wardrobe cartons can be purchased. When full, these boxes can weigh 70-100 pounds. In addition to being heavy, the box alone costs about $12. Therefore, seriously consider dumping all clothing which is badly worn out or outdated. If there are suits with real wide lapels, try flapping them vigorously for a few minutes. If the lapels are big enough, maybe you can fly to your new home very economically!

Firewood, Lumber. They both are "no-no's" unless you have an abundance of money to transport these heavy items.

Flammables, Pressurized Containers, Combustibles, Explosives, Etc. All categories are "no-no's". The inside of a truck can get extremely hot, since there are no windows for ventilation. All types of aerosol cans (even deodorants, hair sprays, shaving cream, etc.) have the potential to explode. All fuel in power tools, lawn mowers, etc. should be drained.

Propane in tanks should also be emptied. If you have a portable outdoor gas grill for cooking, light the grill a few days before moving (with the top open, of course). Allow the propane to totally burn itself out. If you try to release the propane gas without lighting the grill, the entire neighborhood will be aware of it.

Food. Try to consume most of the food items before the packing begins. Canned goods are heavy and costly to transport. Limit the amount of food, and consider putting spices and lighter things in plastic sandwich bags, instead of heavy jars.

Furniture. It is important to *assess what your needs will be at the new residence.* This takes time and a lot of common sense. For example, if you are moving from a four-bedroom home into a two-bedroom apartment, you will probably have less space for storage. You will have fewer closets, less space in the garage and, or attic, and no basement. Unless you want your new home to resemble a rummage sale, you had better sell the unneeded furniture. Also, if the room sizes are smaller, you might not have room for 3 sofas, 2 loveseats and 4 upholstered chairs.

When going through these deliberations, consider what you *really need*, as well as what you *realistically have room to accommodate*. Both considerations are equally important throughout the entire weeding-out process. A floorplan, along with room dimensions in the new home, will prove to be valuable. If possible, ask the present owner, tenant, or real estate agent to send a copy.

Magazines. If you have an abundance, thumb through the ones that can be eliminated. "Let your scissors do the walking!" Cut out the recipes, articles or pictures of interest. It is time well spent, since a few hundred magazines can be reduced to one small box. This can save some bucks!

Piano, Organ. Only if you cannot live without it, and there is adequate space for proper placement. Since they are heavy, they will be expensive to move. In addition, you should expect to pay a handling charge, and the cost to have it retuned at destination.

Plants. (Read section called "Transporting Plants".)

Pool Table. Only if you still use it; only if there is a room that it will comfortably fit into; only if it is worth the cost of transportation and special handling charges. If it has a slate surface, it should be completely disassembled. For safety, the slate should be placed in a wooden crate. At destination, someone will have to reassemble the pieces. It can be an expensive endeavor.

Telephone Book. Pack the telephone book from your present community. You will be surprised to discover how helpful it will be in the future. Most people discard it, then a year later, need to find an address or telephone number for some sort of communication. It can be especially useful during a holiday season when you need addresses for sending greeting cards.

Things attached to walls, ceilings. In general, items attached to walls or ceilings are usually better off staying there. They look attractive while attached, and can increase the total amount you are able to sell or rent the house for. Once removed, the area left behind can often resemble a wall or ceiling that was used for target practice with a shotgun. Also, before removing anything attached to the house, be sure you are legally permitted to do so. Items such as ceiling fans, built-in shelving, lighting fixtures, outdoor TV antennas, etc. are sometimes not included in the sale of a house.

Tools. Since they are extremely heavy, you will have to decide if you really need 5 hammers, 25 screwdrivers and 10 pairs of pliers. If you have accumulated an abundance of duplicate tools, try to eliminate the ones in the worst condition. It only takes one hammer to drive a nail into a piece of wood. Plus, when was the last time you broke a hammer?

If you are driving a car to the new location, place your toolbox in the trunk. That translates into 50 pounds of weight you are not paying to move, and it can be useful in an emergency. Lastly, since you will probably arrive at destination before the truck, the tools will be handy for odd jobs that need immediate attention.

Valuables. Do not include as part of the shipment. Make separate arrangements for their transportation. (Read the section explaining "liability protection" for further information on this subject.)

THE PROFESSIONAL PACK JOB

It's definitely a real treat to have experienced, professional packers perform the entire job. It is also interesting to watch. However, it can also be expensive. You will pay for each box provided, as well as a separate labor charge, based on the size of each container.

If you request the company to pack everything, it will usually send 1 or 2 packers on the day prior to the truck's arrival (unless a weekend or holiday is involved). They will pack everything, except items you need to use until the truck arrives. If requested, the packers will leave a few boxes behind which the driver can finish packing. Boxspring and mattress containers, a wardrobe box, and maybe a box in the kitchen are typical examples. (By the way, it is a good idea to plan on dining out the night before departure.)

The price for a professional pack job can be drastically reduced if you are willing to do some of the work. Non-breakable items such as books, tools, pots and pans, tupperware, silverware, linens, bedding and clothing are easy to do. Just packing these items yourself can drastically cut the packing cost.

You may request the company to only pack items of a fragile nature (china, crystal, glassware, lamp bases, pictures, mirrors, bric-a-brac, etc.). Not only is this convenient and safe, but it also helps to avoid a battle later on if a damage claim needs to be filed. If you did the packing, the "Was it packed properly?" question usually will surface with the moving company claims department. (Read the section on "liability coverage" for more details.)

THE DO-IT-YOURSELF PACK JOB

Packing is not a difficult chore. It requires some common sense, proper supplies, adequate planning, and a whole lot of time. It's a good idea to start packing a few boxes each day, at least one month prior to the move. Slowly whittle away at items that will not be needed during that time. You should be able to live without most items in the garage, attic, and basement. Many of the things contained in cupboards and closets can be placed in boxes a few weeks prior to moving. Designate an area in the garage, or in a spare room, for stacking the boxes.

During the last month, you will have prospective purchasers or tenants, neighbors, friends, and family members cruising through the house. Your goal is to have the residence appear as normal as possible. Pictures and wall decorations should remain hanging until a few days before the move.

Tell all family members that once they start packing a box, they should finish the job and place the box in the designated area. It can be very unsightly and embarrassing to have visitors walk by a room with assorted piles of "stuff" covering every inch of floor space. If you do not try to control the situation from the very beginning, your quaint home may look like General Sherman and his troops just rode through!

OBTAINING BOXES

There are a few ways to cut the cost of purchasing boxes, without sacrificing safety. However, you must start the "box shopping" routine a few months ahead of time. *This step can often reduce the total moving cost by $300-$400.*

The best place to obtain free, sturdy boxes is at the local liquor store. Since these boxes are designed to carry the weight of heavy liquor bottles, they are prefect for packing books, tools, silverware, and even your delicate glassware. (Many have cardboard dividers in them.)

You will need to "cut a deal" with an employee. Ask which day they receive most of their deliveries and stock the shelves. That is the best time to return. Since most stores have very limited storage space, they will usually cut the tops off of boxes, crush them, and throw them into a dumpster. Unless you receive a prior commitment, most stores will not have a nice variety to choose from. *Select only sturdy boxes with tops,* since all containers will need to be sealed shut and stacked.

Supermarkets also want to get boxes out of their way. As soon as the contents go on a shelf, the box is cut and thrown out. Prior arrangements should also be made at these stores. You can usually obtain some larger-sized boxes at a supermarket, but make sure they are sturdy. If they are not, do not use them. You do not want a truck full of accordions unloaded at destination. You will sometimes find fruit boxes with telescoping tops and bottoms. They are usually sturdy and can be used for larger-sized items.

Large stores such as Costco, Sam's Club, Staples, Office Depot and Smart & Final are also good sources for small boxes. Cartons used to deliver heavy products are usually sturdy.

Friends, neighbors, and relatives are great sources. Many people collect boxes in their garage, attic or basement areas for use sometime in the future. After a few years, they accumulate an abundant supply for which they probably have no immediate or long

"Remember, only the *empty* boxes are free!"

range plans to use. Ask to partially "tap into their stash" since it can always be replenished.

Technically, it is illegal for a moving company to give "free-bees" to a customer, "as a condition for doing business" on an interstate move. It is considered an illegal "rebate". However, some companies pile discarded, used boxes outside of their warehouse. They acquire them from people who request unpacking. When an employer is paying for a relocation, this request is fairly common. When the driver goes to the local warehouse to return his paperwork, he usually has some used boxes to contribute to the pile. It may be beneficial to drive by a few moving companies to see if they have an assortment of discarded boxes. The trip could save you a lot of time and money if it is fruitful. "Nothing ventured, nothing gained!"

If you must purchase boxes from a moving company, you should expect to pay a hefty price for cardboard. It is most convenient, but also most expensive. You may want to limit these purchases to mattress and wardrobe boxes. They are very bulky, cumbersome, and difficult to transport with a car.

There are a few cheaper sources available if you must purchase them. Some of the larger truck rental agencies sell boxes and other types of packing supplies. Their prices are usually lower than those of the moving companies. Thumb through your local Yellow Pages under the "Moving-Truck Rental" section. Call a few agencies to get an idea of prices. If you need a large supply, they are sometimes cheaper "by the dozen".

Another source is available when a large supply of containers is needed. It is sometimes possible to purchase boxes directly from the companies that manufacture and distribute them. Look in the Yellow Pages under "Containers, Corrugated". Be sure to call before going to their place of business, since many do not sell directly to the public. Also, some may have a minimum amount that must be purchased.

SETTING UP SHOP (SUPPLIES NEEDED)

One secret to packing like the professionals is to have the proper materials and an organized environment. Without the proper "tools", the completed job will be mediocre at best.

Using the kitchen table as a work area is usually most convenient. When packing in rooms which are quite a distance from the kitchen, use a card table as your portable work station. Tape plastic to the surface of the table. It will prevent ink on the newspaper from rubbing off and soiling the surface.

Newspaper. If you do not mind having black hands at the end of the process, newspaper is still a cheap and effective packing material to use. It is the same type of paper used by the professionals, except the paper has ink on it. Since it does smudge, certain precautions need to be taken. As long as the newsprint does not directly touch the items being packed, damage from the ink should not occur. The trick is explained next!

Trash Bags, Baggies. Buy a healthy supply of large sandwich bags and various-sized trash bags. They can be used for all items that can be soiled by newspaper ink. Linens, clothing, small appliances, and lamp shades are typical examples. Dishes and glassware can be pre-wrapped in small plastic bags to eliminate the need to wash them when unpacked. These bags can also be used for packing food items, and for small amounts of nails, screws, nuts, bolts, etc.

Twist-Ties. Use the leftovers from a package of trash bags to secure all electrical cords on small appliances.

Bubble Wrap, "Peanuts". If you buy special styrofoam products, use them only on the more valuable and delicate possessions. For most of your packing needs, newspaper is just fine.

Tissue Paper. Should be used instead of plastic bags for packing silverware and other silver items. Do not allow newspaper to directly touch silver.

111

Tape. The easiest to use is the 2″-3″ wide plastic tape. It also provides the strength needed to adhere to a variety of surfaces. The tape that needs to be moistened with water is cumbersome to use, and will not hold as much weight. Masking tape is not as strong as the plastic variety, and tends to "get unglued" in a warm climate.

Razor Blade Knife. Can be used for cutting tape and also to cut cardboard when constructing an odd-shaped box. It's easier to use than a pair of scissors.

Felt-Tip Marker. Get a few different colors for writing the contents, as well as "special instructions" on the sides of each box ("This Side Up", "Fragile", etc.).

PROPER LABELING

Once a box is packed, use a felt-tip marker to indicate which room it will be placed in, and to itemize its contents. If the professionals do the packing, work along with them to be sure the contents of each box gets itemized on the *side of the container*. They will only make general notations such as "master bedroom - linens". You want to place your own list of contents on the side of each box, since some may need to be stored alongside a wall in the new basement, garage or attic area.

A common mistake is to make notations on the top of a box. Once they are stacked on top of each other, the notations are no longer visible. You are forced to shuffle them around in order to find the exact one desired. This can be time-consuming and rough on your back muscles.

On moving day, the movers will place inventory numbers on all boxes and other items to be loaded on the truck. These labels do not describe the contents or corresponding room locations where boxes should be placed at destination. To save yourself and the movers a lot of time, aggravation, and extra work, make sure each box is clearly labeled explaining room location and contents.

Avoid using the word "miscellaneous" to describe contents

Labeling - List the contents on the side of each box.
Also, be sure each container gets an inventory sticker.

of a container. If you don't know how to describe your 25-year old collection of unneeded, unwanted, unused and ugly Christmas gifts, then simply use the description just mentioned. If "miscellaneous" is written on the box, you are sure to open it a few times each year while looking for something else. That kind of surprise, you don't need!

Several of the larger interstate moving companies provide free gummed labels that are contained in their informational booklets. They say "Fragile", "Do Not Load", etc. Ask each representative for a booklet explaining the company's services.

TYPICAL BOX SIZES

Small Box (1.5 cubic feet) - 13″ X 13″ X 16″ - Commonly referred to as a "book carton". It is ideal for small, heavy items (books, paper products, canned goods, small appliances, tools, etc.). If you pack any of these items in a large box, the bottom may fall out when lifted. Cardboard and tape are not strong enough to hold an excessive amount of weight. If you "over-pack" a box and the bottom falls out, it will be tough to blame the movers. Remember the old adage, "A word to the wise should be sufficient!"

Medium Box (3 cubic feet) - 18″ X 18″ X 16″ - This size is twice the size of the small box (book carton). It should be used to pack most of what remains (except large items), after the heavy items are placed in the small boxes. Typical examples are pots, pans, kitchen items, shoes, purses, garden supplies, toys, etc.

Even though there is a specially designed "dish-pak" container available for packing dishes and glassware, you may want to consider using medium or small boxes. If you are an inexperienced packer, it is easy to make the mistake of placing certain types of fragile items at the bottom of a "dish-pak", which cannot endure the excessive weight (70 pounds) on top of them.

Large box (4.5 cubic feet) - 18″ X 18″ X 24″ - Should be used for light-weight, bulky items such as lamp shades, pillows, blankets, bedspreads, etc. Avoid placing fragile items in this size box since it is not as sturdy as a "dish-pak".

Dish-pak (6 cubic feet) - 18″ X 18″ X 30″ - This is specially constructed to hold the weight of heavy, fragile items. The cardboard is twice the thickness of a normal box. It usually includes cardboard dividers to separate each item, and can be used for fragile items such as lamp bases, dishes, china and glassware.

Mirror, Picture Box - A telescoping carton that can be adjusted to protect glass, mirrors, pictures and paintings. (For extremely delicate or larger items, specially constructed wooden crates should be utilized.)

Wardrobe Box - 21″ X 24″ X 48″ - A huge box with a metal bar (approximately 2 feet) extending across the top. Clothing presently hanging in closets can stay on the hangers. It eliminates the need to spend endless hours ironing clothes at destination. It can also eliminate a huge dry-cleaning bill for suits and dresses. If curtains, draperies or hanging plants need to be packed, this box is the answer.

It is also great for tall objects that will not fit into other containers. In addition, you will sometimes have unused space at the bottom which can be used for pillows, shoe boxes, or other lightweight items. That means a few less boxes you need to buy.

Mattress/Boxspring Carton - These boxes are individually designed to fit various bed sizes. They protect against soiling and snags. It is easy to rip the bottom of a boxspring that has a thin fabric stretched over the wooden frame.

If it happens to be raining at the time of loading or unloading, the moisture may cause a mattress/boxspring to acquire a musty odor that can linger for months. The box helps to prevent this from occurring.

There is another benefit to using these boxes. They allow the movers to pack the truck with less likelihood of damage occurring to other items. They reduce the possibility of movement inside the truck due to bumps and road vibrations.

INDIVIDUAL CONSIDERATIONS

The following is a list of common household items that require packing or special attention. Continue to refer back to this section throughout the entire process.

Aerosol Cans, Paints, Explosives, or Anything Flammable - All categories are illegal to transport on an interstate shipment, when using the professionals. If you pack them in a box and try to sneak them on the truck, you will probably be liable for any damage that may result. These are definite candidates to sell or give away before moving.

Air Conditioner - Before you decide to take it, be sure the new residence has proper electrical wiring to accommodate the unit. Also, check the owner's manual to find out if any special parts need to be secured (compressor, etc.). If you cannot find the manual, try calling a local appliance dealer for recommendations.

Appliances (small kitchen items such as a toaster, blender, iron, food processor, etc.) - Place in a small box. Pack in an upright position after prewrapping in a small plastic or paper bag. Do not allow newspaper to come in direct contact with the item. If bags are not available, prewrap in tissue paper, then use regular newspaper to finish the job. Secure all electrical cords with a "twist-tie".

It is most convenient to pack all small appliances into the same boxes. It makes unpacking much easier to organize. Kitchen towels can be used to fill open areas in these boxes.

Barbeque (Propane Gas) - Before disassembling, light the grill (with top up) a few days beforehand. Allow the propane to "burn itself out".

Clean extra thoroughly to get rid of grease build-up. Place detachable parts and briquets into plastic bags. Put bags into a small box along with garden tools, etc.

Beds (Also see "Mattress, Boxspring") - Even though the movers will usually disassemble and reassemble regular bedframes, you may want to take the rails off before they arrive. This allows you to label each rail so they are placed in the correct position at destination. The rails and the crosspieces should be tied together with rope or tape.

If you have bunkbeds or a waterbed that needs to be disassembled, do this on the morning of your move. Professional movers will not usually disassemble these beds, unless you are willing to pay an extra labor charge.

Bicycles, Tricycles - Clean thoroughly and wipe off grease deposits that usually accumulate near the chain. Since they are awkward to pack inside a truck, slightly loosen the handlebars so they can be turned.

Books - Place them flat, in small sturdy boxes. Always alternate the bindings (spine) of hard-covered books. This helps to prevent the glue in the bindings from cracking. Stuff newspaper into open spaces to avoid movement.

If you have a large collection of books, read sub-section entitled "Using the Post Office" for possible money-saving ideas.

Bottles, Glass Jars - (See "Food" section.)

Cedar Chest, Trunk, Footlocker - There is no need to empty the contents, unless it contains fragile or heavy items. Fill with linens, bedspreads, comforters, towels, sweaters, etc. If the contents are not going to be immediately unpacked at destination, place mothballs inside.

China Cabinet - All removable shelving needs to be taken out. Glass shelves must be boxed. Wooden ones can be bundled and stood on end in a wardrobe container. If the doors can be locked, they should be. The drawers and storage space below can be used to pack towels and small pillows.

Clocks - Remove the pendulum, if possible, from grandfather, grandmother, and mantle clocks. Place the pendulum and other removable hardware (weights) in a separate box. If you have an older mantle clock that is very heavy, pack tightly in a small box by itself.

Clothes Hamper - If you plan on taking it, fill it with linens, towels, shoe boxes, pillows, etc. Then tape it shut like a box, if you can do so without causing damage to the finish.

Clothing (Hanging) - Wardrobe cartons are a real blessing. Be sure to use them. Face the hangers in the same direction on the bar. It will make unpacking much easier.

For all clothing and fabric items which will not be used immediately upon arrival at destination (especially seasonal items), put mothballs in the containers. If you have limited closet space in the new home, these wardrobe boxes can be used for storage of seasonal clothing in an attic or garage.

If a dresser is extremely heavy and needs to be maneuvered up or down stairs or in an elevator, drawers should then be emptied.

If the dresser is placed in storage, put moth balls in each drawer. When being stored for a long period of time, it is wise to pack clothing in sealed boxes. In either case, remember that it is better to have clothing smell like moth balls, than look like Swiss cheese!

Do not use tape or rope to prevent drawers or doors from opening. The tape can stick to the surface and harm the finish. Also, constant rubbing from the rope can cause damage. The movers should place furniture pads (blankets) over each piece of furniture. Then, large "rubber bands" are used to hold the blankets in place. They resemble the inner-tube from a bicycle. This procedure should adequately secure the drawers and doors.

Clothing (Boxed) – Most clothing can be placed into medium-sized boxes. Avoid using newspaper, unless plastic bags are used first. Road vibrations over a long distance can magically transform a white shirt into a gray one!

Curtains, Draperies, Window Treatments – Usually they are left behind for the new occupants to enjoy. It is unlikely you will have the exact size window and same color scheme in the new residence. If you decide to move them, consider leaving the shades intact. The new occupants will appreciate not having to tape newspaper or sheets over the windows.

If curtains and drapes are transported, place them on a hanger and hang in a wardrobe carton. This can save a few hours of standing in front of an ironing board at destination.

Curtain Rods – They should be tied in a small bundle. Small pieces of hardware can be put into little plastic bags and taped to each rod. If possible, stand the bundle on end, inside a wardrobe carton. Place a tall piece of cardboard next to any clothing to avoid the possibility of a snag.

Desk - For drawers containing small objects and, or office supplies, pack the contents in a box since these items will be jostled around. Unless the desk is extremely heavy, other drawers can be left intact. Simply stuff towels or newspaper in the drawers to prevent movement.

Dishes, Glasses, China - When packing all items that are breakable in nature, remember to "paper everything to death". Start by putting a few inches of wadded-up paper along the bottom, before you even begin. Place the heaviest items, individually wrapped in paper, at the very bottom (platters, large bowls, etc.). Save the more delicate pieces to pack in the upper layers. If you have a few small items (heavy sugar bowls, salt and pepper shakers, etc.), use them to fill the open spaces. Of course, even these small articles will need to be wrapped in paper. Never pack unwrapped items inside each other.

If you are using a dish-pak, you should have four or more layers when you are done. If a smaller-sized box is used, at least two layers will probably result. Place wadded-up newspaper in between each layer to make it level and to provide cushioning. Dish towels, bath towels, and wash cloths can also be used for this purpose.

After packing the bottom layer with large bowls and platters, the next layer should contain large dishes. After that, the next layer should be smaller plates and saucers. The top layer should be reserved for the more delicate items.

Dishes, plates and saucers should be individually wrapped, then packaged together in bundles. After placing four or five similar-sized items in a bundle, wrap a few sheets of paper around the bundle to hold it together. *Always pack dishes, plates and saucers standing on edge in a box. Do not lay them flat!* This may sound strange, but there is less chance of damage when they are packed in an upright position. If you pack them on top of each other, in a flat position, the ones at the bottom of the pile may be subjected to more weight than they can handle.

Cups and glasses should be placed upside down (on their rims), after being individually wrapped in paper. If they are similar in size, you can "nest" three or four glasses together to form a bundle. Always prewrap each one, using a few small pieces of paper. You never want to have "glass-on-glass".

Stemware and figurines should be packed in dish-paks and, or cartons retrieved from a liquor store. They usually have cardboard inserts (dividers) that can be used to separate stemware, goblets and glasses. After each piece is individually wrapped, it should be placed upside down in a cubicle. If any space is left at the top of a cubicle, stuff paper in the open area.

With delicate pieces of stemware, avoid placing too much pressure on the base. Put tissue paper inside the goblet and around the stem, before wrapping in newspaper.

Always mark in bold print, on the side of a box containing fragile items, "Fragile-Glass" and draw arrows showing which end should stay in an upright position. Also, state "This Side Up" on each side of the container. You do not want these boxes placed on the truck in any position other than the way they were packed.

Dressers (Also see "Clothing-In Dressers") - Remove attached mirrors, and place into mirror cartons, glass packs. If the casters come off easily, remove them. Place the screws and other hardware in a plastic bag. Then, tape the bag to the inside of a drawer.

Dryer (Clothes)- (Read section on "Washer (Clothes)", and also refer to "Extras" section for additional information.)

Fans, Portable Heaters - If they are small enough to fit in a box, place them in one. Since the original box is probably constructed of thin cardboard, consolidate these small boxes into one sturdy container. Even if you are relocating to a warm climate, do not discard these items. They will be useful in the future.

Filing Cabinet - Dump the contents no longer needed. If the drawers contain a metal plate that can be moved forward, position it so that the paperwork cannot move. If the cabinet can be locked to prevent the drawers from opening, do so.

Fireplace Tools - Thoroughly wash, bundle and place in a box. If you pack them in a box containing other living room items, be sure to prewrap in a plastic bag. Consider placing in a box containing your odd-shaped garden tools, etc.

Food - Consume as much as possible before packing begins. Discard all perishables and the opened jars, cans. Remaining canned goods should be placed at the bottom of a small or medium-sized box. Dry goods can be placed at the top. Use newspaper between layers.

Glass jars, bottles should be individually wrapped in newspaper. Make sure all lids are tightly secured. Use tape to prevent opening due to road vibrations. It is a good idea to put liquid food containers into plastic sandwich bags, before placing in a box. Stuff newspaper into unfilled areas. You do not want maple syrup covering the contents, or leaking out of the box!

If your shipment is going to be stored for a long period of time, consider dumping all food items. Otherwise, you may have boxes full of moldy food or bugs greeting you in your new home.

Furniture (Small Articles) - The general rule-of-thumb is "if it will conveniently fit into a box, put it in one!" The movers want as much uniformity as possible, to fit everything tightly on the truck. They pack the inside of a truck like you would pack a box. Small, oddshaped items make it very difficult. Articles such as magazine, wine racks, stacking tables that disassemble, small plant stands, etc. should go into boxes.

Garden Hose, Tools - Thoroughly drain the hose, and screw one end into the other. Then, put into a medium-sized box or trash can with other small garden tools. Long-handled garden tools (rakes, shovels, brooms, etc.) should be tied or taped in bundles.

Lamp Base (Table) - Tall, narrow boxes can be purchased that are specially made for large table lamps. A dish-pak container can also be used, especially if there are several lamp bases that can be packed into one box.

Remove the lightbulb, shade and the "harp" that the shade rests on (if it removes easily). The electrical cord can be wrapped around the base.

Place a generous supply of wadded-up newspaper at the bottom of the box to act as a cushion. Wrap several sheets of paper around the entire base. Then, fold down excess paper at the top and bottom so that it is completely covered. Tape down the top, bottom, and all sides to hold paper in place.

When there are several bases being packed into one box, alternate the top of one with the bottom of another. This helps to get a tighter fit inside the box. Place wadded-up paper along the sides, and in any open areas of the box to prevent movement. Do not pack dishes or other heavy breakable items on top of the bases if they are laid in a flat position. As a matter of fact, if they can be placed in a vertical position, they are better off.

Use plenty of newspaper, just as you would when packing dishes, glassware or china. Don't be skimpy! Be sure to write "Fragile" and "This Side Up" on each side of the box.

Lamp Shades - Remove all shades, light bulbs, and metal shadeholders, if possible. Place shades in separate boxes, nesting smaller ones inside the larger ones. Do not use newspaper and do not pack other miscellaneous items into these boxes. The fabric can be easily dented, ripped, crushed, and soiled. Place each shade into a plastic bag, or use tissue paper to protect it.

When handling a lamp shade, always use the metal frame on top to avoid fingerprint marks. After packing other items, you are bound to have dirty hands. These stains will be very difficult to remove without harming the shade. Write "Fragile - Lamp Shades" on all sides of each box.

Lamp (Floor) - Remove shade and light bulb. The electrical cord can be wrapped around the base, or gathered together and tied with a twist-tie. Some floor lamps can be easily disassembled and placed in a box. Look for a metal nut under the base that can be removed.

Lawn Mower (Gas) - Gas and oil should be removed. Allow the motor to run until gas is gone. Leave the gas cap off for awhile. Drain the oil and detach the handle. Place the mower into a trash bag to prevent damage from leakage.

Linens (Towels, Sheets, Blankets) - Can be placed in drawers, as long as the furniture items do not become too heavy. Can also be used for packing. Use plastic bags or tissue paper to prevent soiling.

Liquor - Illegal to transport on an interstate shipment of household goods.

Mattress, Boxspring - Should be placed in special boxes that can be purchased from a moving company. Leave the slip covers on. They are easy to take off and put into a washer. Nobody has been ingenious enough to figure out a convenient method of placing a soiled mattress into a washer!

Microwave Oven - Pack it in the original box if you have it. If not, it can go the way it is. The movers will wrap a furniture pad around it.

Night Table - Remove all breakables. Stuff newspaper or towels into the top drawer so that the contents cannot move. If the bottom area has a door, place linen items inside. Since these tables are small, they will not get ridiculously heavy when packed.

Pictures (Small) - Should be individually wrapped, then placed side-by-side in the same box. Do not put one on top of the other. Use a sheet of tissue paper or plastic if the newsprint can smudge the picture. Stuff newspaper into open areas to prevent movement.

Pictures, Mirrors (Large) - Should be tightly packed into special boxes called "glass packs" or "mirror cartons". Use wide tape to criss-cross a large glass or mirrored surface. This helps to prevent breakage due to road vibrations.

Make-shift cardboard containers may be constructed from left-over cardboard boxes. If this is done, use plenty of paper to prevent movement, and to prevent the edges of the frame from being exposed. You do not want scratches on the frame, or the corners left on the front lawn!

Write "Glass-Fragile" on both sides of each container. Always place these boxes in an upright position, and never lay flat.

Special wooden crates should be used for extremely large pieces of glass or marble, valuable art work, delicate frames, etc. You can pay to have the moving company construct the crate, or do it yourself. Since getting a proper fit can be tricky for the do-it-yourselfer, find out what the cost would be to have it done professionally. It may be worth it.

For pictures, paintings, prints and frames of high value, describe separately and declare a value on all copies of the inventory. A photograph and an appraisal is highly recommended.

Pots, Pans - Place in medium-sized boxes using plenty of paper. Put a layer of wadded paper on the bottom. Individually wrap each item, then put more paper into any open spaces. Avoid a "shake, rattle, and roll" situation once the box is moved. Plus, do not pack any fragile items into these boxes.

Refrigerator, Freezer - Unplug about 48 hours prior to loading.

Hopefully, you will have consumed or given away most of your food items by that time. Periodically, inspect the water tray under the appliance, and carefully empty as needed. You do not want a puddle of water to accumulate underneath. If it does, you can bet damage to the flooring will occur. Also, when the movers tilt the appliance to place it on a dolly, you do not want a trail of water dripping all the way out the door.

An automatic ice-making machine should be drained and properly disconnected from a refrigerator. Check the owner's manual for instructions, or consult with a professional appliance serviceman. Other precautions may also be necessary for your particular appliance.

Remove all shelving and trays, and pack separately in a box. Once the appliance is totally defrosted and drained, clean and dry thoroughly. Use paper towels to remove excess water. Leave the doors open, allowing all moisture to evaporate.

If you have small children, an emptied refrigerator/freezer can become a real hazard. Use rope to tie the door shut, after placing a block of wood inside to keep the door slightly open. In addition, advise your children to stay out of the room where the appliance is located.

Once the appliance is totally clean and dry, place baking soda inside to absorb musty odors. Coffee grounds or charcoal can also be used, but are messy to clean up. If you sprinkle baking soda on the bottom of each compartment, a damp sponge is all that is necessary at destination. If you insist on using coffee grounds or charcoal, use panty-hose or a nylon stocking for a container. Cut into sections, then tie a knot at both ends.

When the appliance is moved away from the wall, coil the electrical cord and tie with a twist-tie. Then, tape the cord to the rear of the appliance. Have cleaning supplies ready to wash the back end, as well as the floor area. It's amazing how much dirt and dust can accumulate through the years!

If you need to move any large appliance away from a wall before the movers arrive, here's a tip to make the job easier. Spray a small amount of liquid glass cleaner on the linoleum floor at each corner that can be reached. This will help to "lubricate" the floor and make the job easier. Wipe up with paper towels when done. Another helpful tip is to place carpet scraps under each leg and pull it along. Since it is easy to damage floors when trying to "jocky" a heavy appliance out of a small area, you may want to wait until the movers do this.

Rugs - You should have rugs cleaned prior to moving day. It is a nice feeling to roll out spotless rugs in a new home.

All large rugs should be rolled up and tied. For added protection, a plastic dropcloth can be placed around the rugs before tying them.

Small rugs should be packed together in a large box. If storage is a possibility use moth balls when rolling up or boxing any rugs.

Sewing Machine (Cabinet) - Remove the machine from the wood cabinet and place in a small box. Usually, it only requires removing a few screws. Place all hardware, bobbins, etc. into a plastic bag and pack into the same box.

Sewing Machine (portable) - Can be placed in small or medium-sized box with other lightweight items. If it has a sturdy case, it is not essential to place in a box.

Shoe, Hat Boxes - Since these boxes are real flimsy, consolidate and place in sturdy boxes. If there is still unused space at the bottom of a wardrobe box, they can be placed there. However, do not overload this area. You do not want the bottom of the wardrobe to fall out.

Silver pieces - Do not allow newspaper or plastic to directly touch silver items. Tissue paper, special silvercloth, or a felt fabric is recommended. Use newspaper only for cushioning around each piece. If you have a silver chest containing tableware, stuff tissue paper inside to tightly secure the contents. Then, place at the bottom of a small box with other items.

If you have silver items of high value, consider packing them into a suitcase that will be traveling with you. If these items go on the truck, describe them separately on all copies of the inventory and declare a value for each item. Having pictures and an appraisal is a good idea. Purchasing the best "valuation coverage" available is highly recommended.

Stove - Thoroughly clean to remove grease build-up. Place removable parts in a box (trays, grates, knobs, etc.). If the burner elements do not easily remove, use tape to secure them.

Gas connections need to be disconnected from the outlet before the movers arrive. If you are unable to do the disconnecting, ask the moving company representative for the name of an appliance specialist whom you can call to provide this service. This should be arranged long before moving day.

Suitcase - Can be used as a packing container for non-breakable items such as sheets, towels, sweaters, etc. That translates into a few less boxes you will need to purchase.

Television - If the original box is still available, use it. If not, pack tightly in a box by itself to prevent damaging the screen or control knobs.

Always keep the television in an upright position. Never lay flat or on its side. Mark on the sides of the box "Fragile - This Side Up", so the movers know how to handle it. Expect to make a few minor adjustments at destination.

Tools - If you have metal or wooden tool chests that can be tightly closed, use them. If not, pack all tools, nails, nuts, bolts, screws, etc.

into small boxes. Plastic bags can be used to separate various sizes.

Cabinets, work benches, and dressers in the garage that are full of heavy items should be emptied. As you are doing so, properly label the outside of the box to make unpacking a breeze.

Tool Chest - If you are driving to the new residence, pack a small tool chest in the trunk. It may be useful on the trip in the event you experience mechanical problems. Most importantly, it will be useful at both ends for little chores that will need to be performed.

Toys - Large plastic toys can be placed in a large box. A clean trash can may be used if it can be tightly taped shut. If you are real industrious, you can individually wrap each item. However, if they are still in one piece, there is not too much the movers can do to these items to damage them!

Vacuum Cleaner - Clean the bag and transport in the trunk of your car, if possible. It is nice to have it available for use before the van arrives. It it does get loaded on the truck, ask the movers to load it last. In doing so, you are certain to have it unloaded before the furniture.

Valuables - Do not include in the shipment. Make separate arrangements to transport coin, stamp collections, valuable documents, jewelry, etc. If you are driving, never leave valuables behind in your automobile or motel room. Keep by your side at all times. There may be other people interested in traveling with your possessions!

Washer (Clothes) - (Also see "Extras" section for additional information) - Disconnect both hoses from faucet. Drain the hoses and allow them to thoroughly dry. If the appliance has a "spring-mounted" motor, it should be secured by "blocking" it. Hoses and the electrical cord should be taped to the back. Check the owner's manual or call an appliance dealer for more specific instructions about your machine.

If this all sounds too complicated, call a serviceman to

perform this task. If you are willing to pay the transportation cost, do not be skimpy when thinking about the additional cost to have any appliance properly prepared for the trip. When all is said and done, you want an appliance to work properly when it arrives at destination.

A styrofoam "washer block" can be purchased from the moving company to prevent the tub from rotating. Towels or folded pieces of cardboard can be tightly wedged into the space between the top of the tub and side walls to provide bracing. This will prevent the tub from bouncing around every time the truck hits a bump in the road.

If you are moving during the winter months, do not use any appliance that circulates hot water until it reaches normal room temperature (wait a few days). When the appliance is cold, real hot water can cause damage. This also applies to dishwashers.

PACKING A "CAR-BOX"

If you are traveling in an automobile, handy items can be placed in a small box on the back seat or floor. Here are some suggestions.

- Aerosol tire inflator
- Camera
- Emergency tools
  (if tool box is not going)
- Flashlight
- Games, toys for children

- Litter bag
- Napkins
- Road Maps
- Snacks
- Sunglasses

Of course, do not forget items that should go in a wallet such as a driver's license, credit cards, car ownership, registration card and insurance card.

PACKING THE "KEEP WITH YOU AT ALL TIMES" SUITCASE

Since valuables should not be included in a shipment of household goods, they always present a transportation problem. If these items are going to accompany you in the car, they can be packed in a suitcase or a box. In either case, do not leave the container unattended. The following is a partial list of what you may need to make special arrangements to transport:

- Bank account books
- Coin, stamp collection
- Currency of any kind
- Insurance policies
- Jewelry
- Medical, dental records
- Precious metals or stones
- School records for children
- Valuable documents

PACKING A "QUICK-FIX BOX"

There are certain things you may need immediately upon arrival at destination. These items should be placed in a box and taken in the car. If you are flying, inquire about checking the box in along with your luggage. For that matter, a suitcase could be used instead of a box! Since you will arrive at the new home before the movers, it will be helpful to have some basic essentials. The trick is to minimize what you have to buy. Limit your purchases to those items which are impractical or dangerous to take. The following is a list of the most common items to pack in your "Quick-Fix Box":

- Alarm clock
- Cleaning supplies (rags, plastic bucket, paper towels, cleanser, glass cleaner, plastic trash bags, disinfectants (non-aerosol)
- Coffee pot (coffee filters, powdered milk, sugar)
- Cooking utensils (paper plates and cups, napkins, plastic glasses and silverware, frying pan, cooking pot, bottle opener, can opener)
- Extension cords

- First aid box (aspirin, band aids)
- Flashlight and candles (take a few, since the electricity may not be turned on)
- Foods (coffee, tea, cereal, salt and pepper)
- Fuses
- Games (a few small items to keep the children out of your hair)
- Light bulbs (an assortment of various sizes)
- Radio with batteries
- Sheets (to cover windows)
- Shelving paper and thumb tacks
- Tape measure
- Toiletries (soap, toilet paper, facial tissues, towels, shampoo)
- Tools (hammer, screwdriver, pliers, wrench, scissors, three-way electrical plug, small assortment of various-sized nails and screws)

SECTION 8
USING THE POST OFFICE
AND OTHER ALTERNATIVES

"Active participation does pay off."
    - Billy and Kristy, after saving big bucks by taking their library of law books to the Post Office.

If you are interested in saving money on a long-distance move and willing to accept a small amount of inconvenience, a variety of alternatives are available for shipping a portion of your household goods.

Some savings can be derived by sending your boxes through either the Post Office; privately owned "parcel carriers"; interstate bus companies; the railroad; or the airlines. Even though they charge according to the weight of a box and the miles traveled (except the airlines), their rates are usually less than an interstate moving company.

Use the telephone book or Internet to find out the current rates, packing requirements, or other conditions each may have. You will discover a big variance on a long-distance move. Find out what kind of insurance is included in their normal rate structure, and the cost for additional coverage you may need. Also, even though you may not be able to include boxes of "breakables" when using a few of these methods, those boxes can be placed on the moving van. As a matter of fact, you should plan on including all boxes containing breakable and fragile items with your shipment of furniture going with the moving company. Remember, the less handling, the less chance of breakage!

133

Most interstate moving companies have a 1000 pound minimum. In addition, the rate for each 100 pounds is extremely high for these shipments. Therefore, if you only need to transport a few furniture pieces and a dozen boxes, you should definitely consider selling the furniture and utilizing an alternate method for shipping the boxes. If you insist on using a moving company, you can expect to "pay the piper".

A few telephone calls and a little "leg-work" can often save hundreds of dollars. You must decide whether any of these methods are appropriate for your situation.

THE POST OFFICE

While the Post Office will ship boxes containing small household items and personal effects, *the biggest bargain can be achieved when books need to be moved.* The government actually gives you a break in this department! When you inquire about rates for shipping books, make sure you ask for the "Special Fourth Class Book Rate".

Using this method can sometimes save more than 50% of the cost of moving books with a moving company (depending on the distance traveled). If you have more than a few boxes, it's definitely worth a trip to the local P.O.

Before preparing books for mailing, check with your local P.O. for the current postage rate. You will be pleasantly surprised to discover that the cost is the same, no matter how many miles the books must travel within the United States.

Once you determine the cost for two 50 pound boxes of books (approximately $37 in 2008), compare that price with the "rate per 100 pounds" that the moving company will be charging to transport books on its truck. Compute the difference in price for every 2 "book cartons" you deliver to the P.O. Then, multiply that amount times every 2 "book cartons" to be shipped. You will soon discover how a little effort on your part can save money if you are moving a long distance.

U.S. POST OFFICE

"What a great way to ship the library!"

P.O. Weight Limitations On Any Box:

Each box is limited to a maximum of 70 pounds. When shipping books, it is doubtful that a box much larger than a "book carton" would be allowed. (When fully packed, it can easily weigh 70 pounds.) In addition, since you have to bring them to the P.O., you do not want them much heavier than 50 pounds.

Use a bathroom scale to be certain you stay within the weight limitation. Don't get stuck repacking boxes at the P.O.

P.O. Size Limitations On Any Box:

They will not accept any box that has a sum total of more than 108 inches. This is calculated by adding the length to what is called the "girth".

Example: A standard size "book carton" used by a moving company is approximately:

17 inches long
13 inches deep (times 2)
13 inches tall (times 2)
69 inches in total

Be sure to label each box, identifying the contents as "BOOKS". Also, keep all shipping receipts. If you qualify to deduct moving expenses on your federal tax return, shipping expenses should be included as a deduction. (See separate section in IRS rules.)

If you have a friend or relative willing to accept boxes at destination, consider shipping them one or two weeks in advance (books take longer to deliver). If you want to personally receive all boxes, drop them off on the day before departure. This should allow enough time for you to travel to destination. Of course, this is assuming you do not take a side trip.

OTHER PARCEL CARRIERS

Throughout the country, independent parcel-shipping companies are available to transport boxes. Some of the most recognized names are United Parcel Service, Fed Ex and GHL. Since there are others performing the same service, it pays to compare prices. They all have weight and size limitations that are similar to the P.O. Like the P.O., they have restrictions on the type of items allowed, as well as packaging requirements. Use the telephone or Internet to inquire about prices, restrictions and packaging information.

In most cities, you can also find "mail centers" that provide various kinds of shipping services. Many are franchise operations which utilize the services of many parcel carriers. While they are usually more conveniently located than the main office of an independent parcel carrier, they usually charge a "handling fee" for each box they process. If you have numerous boxes, driving to the carrier's main office can save a few dollars on each box. However, if you must rent a truck or drive a substantial distance, it may not be worth the trip.

Most independent parcel carriers can usually deliver boxes within one to five days, depending on distance traveled. Therefore, you may want to have someone else receive them at destination if you are planning a leisurely drive by automobile.

U.P.S. provides free "valuation coverage" up to $100 per box. Additional coverage can be purchased at a cost of 25 cents for each additional $100 of declared value. Be sure to ask each company about its coverage. If something is worth the cost of shipping, it is worth protecting against loss or damage.

BUS COMPANIES

This alternative is also worth investigating, especially if you need to transport boxes weighing more than 70 pounds and/or larger than 108 total inches. One of the larger interstate companies which will transport boxes is Greyhound. Of course, you will have to make arrangements to pick up the shipment at a terminal. It does not provide door-to-door service. Information is available at Greyhound "Package Express" at (800) 739-5020 or www.shipgreyhound.com.

Again, use the telephone to inquire about prices, rules and regulations. While each company is slightly different, they all base their prices on weight, distance and size of the boxes. One company may ship boxes which are up to 100 pounds and 141 total inches, and another may transport 150 pound boxes which are even larger. Some will transport boxes containing furniture and "breakable" items, and some will not. With some companies, the price for each box will go down as the total number of boxes increases. For example, from one to ten boxes may be a certain amount, but ten or more may be cheaper for each box. Be sure to ask questions!

USING THE RAILROAD

Interstate railroad companies are another alternative for transporting boxes. Like the bus companies, they will ship "station-to-station". You will need to make arrangements for pickup at their facility. Having a friend available who has a pick-up truck or small van is always helpful.

Amtrak Package Express is one of the larger companies which is capable of shipping boxes from one end of the country to the other. Even though it will ship a box up to three feet long and three feet in width, it must not weigh more than fifty pounds. In addition, it has a 500 pound maximum for each shipment. Since it has restrictions on what is allowed in boxes (no "breakable" or fragile pieces, furniture or appliances, etc.), call to get details before going to the terminal. Call (800) 377-6914 or go to www.amtrak.com.

Like the moving companies, railroads also charge according to the weight and distance traveled. However, the good news is that their rates for each 100 pounds can often be one-half the price. Shipping 500 pounds of boxed items (non-breakable) across the country can translate into hundreds of dollars in savings.

AIRLINES

Each airline has its own set of regulations pertaining to the number of "pieces" allowed, as well as size and weight limitations. If you plan on flying, a telephone call to the airline office can often save money. Today, some airlines are trying to make extra money by charging for a second "piece". Therefore, ask how many "pieces" each member of the family (even children) is entitled to check-in as baggage.

Let's assume that four tickets are purchased and each ticket entitles a person to 2 "pieces" of baggage. If you only have four suitcases, then four boxes may be entitled to a "free ride". If each box weighs 50 pounds, that means 200 pounds are not being loaded on the moving van. If you are paying a transportation rate of $50 for each 100 pounds, you just saved $100 by checking in four boxes at the baggage counter.

Once you determine how many "freebees" you may be entitled to, ask what the additional cost will be for each box that exceeds the limit. Let the airline know your intentions, and find out what procedures to follow at check-in time.

Some airlines offer a very inexpensive method for transporting boxes. However, the major problem is that you are forced to deal with the "hustle and bustle" at airports. You can usually obtain "curb service" by rewarding a porter with a reasonable tip! However, you will need a reliable person with a small van or pick-up truck to offer assistance at both ends of the trip. A taxi cab will not work.

If these details can be easily arranged, find out when you should have everything checked in. Normally, it is two hours prior to departure. If you are not driving to the airport in the same vehicle as your luggage and boxes, have the other vehicle follow you. You want to arrive at the "curb" at the same time. Allow enough time to avoid last-minute anxiety and nervousness, especially if you are traveling with children!

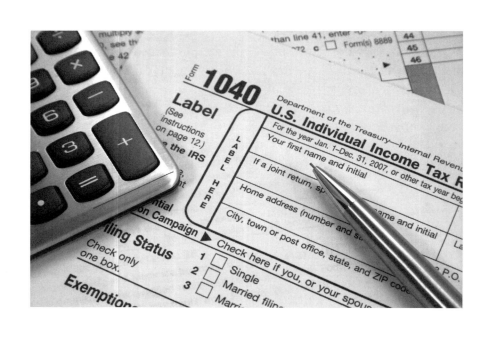

SECTION 9
TAX TIPS

"It is always a pain in the neck, but at least the federal government helps me get the kinks out."
-"Quiet" Bill, a corporate executive who has relocated his family five times in the past twelve years.

If you meet conditions established by the Internal Revenue Service, the federal government may soon become your best friend. However, when dealing with the IRS, you must always keep careful records of everything. Keep written receipts of all moving-related expenses before, during, and after the relocation.

Your tax advisor, or the local IRS office, will help to advise and decipher the deductions to which you may be entitled. There are many exceptions and "special circumstances" that can be applicable. Also, tax laws are frequently revised and changed.

Since the author is not an accountant, attorney, or expert on tax law, only general information and/or excerpts directly taken from IRS publications are provided in this section (IRS Publication #521 and Form #3903 provide complete explanations). Both can be obtained from your local IRS office. Also, your local Post Office or Public Library may stock these publications. On the Internet, you can obtain forms and other information at www.IRS.gov.

Here are some of the categories which are included in IRS Form #3903. Remember, there are many exceptions and special situations that may apply to you.

"Who may deduct moving expenses?" – If you moved your residence because of a change in location of your job, you may be able to deduct your moving expenses. You may qualify for a deduction whether you are self-employed or an employee. However, you must meet certain tests of distance and time.

"Distance Test" – Your new workplace must be at least 50 miles farther from your old residence than the location of your previous workplace. For example, if your old workplace was 3 miles from your old residence, your new workplace must be at least 53 miles from that residence. If you did not have an old workplace, your new workplace must be at least 50 miles from your old residence.

"Time Test" - If you are an employee, you must work full-time for at least 39 weeks during the 12 months right after you move. If you are self-employed, you must work full-time for at least 39 weeks during the first 12 months and a total of at least 78 weeks during the 24 months right after you move.

Different rules may apply if you are a member of the Armed Forces or a retiree or survivor moving to the U.S. (See Publication #521 for specifics).

"Moving Expenses in General – You may deduct most, but not all of the reasonable expenses you incur in moving your family and dependent household members. You may not include moving expenses for employees such as a servant or nurse."

Examples of expenses you MAY deduct are:
- Travel – Lodging expenses during the move to the new residence
- Temporary living expenses in the new location
- Pre-move travel expenses

Examples of expenses you MAY NOT deduct are:
- Meals
- Loss on the sale of your residence
- Mortgage penalties
- Cost of refitting carpets and draperies

- Losses on quitting club memberships

Types of deductions allowed for moving your household goods and personal effects include: cost of packing, moving, crating, storage-in-transit, and insuring your possessions (liability coverage). Also, you may deduct the cost of transporting your car to the new location. There is no dollar limit to these types of deductions! You may include most of the costs to sell or buy a residence or to settle or get a lease.

Examples of expenses you MAY include are:

- Sales commissions
- Advertising costs
- Attorney fees
- Title and escrow fees

"They won't believe I actually have *good* news!"

- State transfer taxes
- Cost to settle an unexpired lease or to get a new lease

Examples of expenses you MAY NOT include are:
- Costs to improve your residence to help it sell
- Charges for payment or prepayment of interest
- Payments or prepayments of rent

Reimbursements - You must include any reimbursements of, or payment for, moving expenses in gross income as compensation for services. If your employer paid for any part of your move, you must report that amount as income on Form 1040 or W-2.

Travel by car. If you use your car to take yourself, members of your household, or your personal effects to your new home, you can figure your expenses by deducting either:
1. Your actual expenses, such as the amount you pay for gas and oil for your car, if you keep an accurate record of each expense, or
2. The standard mileage rate (19 cents a mile).

Whether you use actual expenses or the standard mileage rate to figure your expenses, you can deduct the parking fees and tolls you pay to move. You cannot deduct any part of general repairs, general maintenance, insurance, or depreciation of your car.

Even though you may have other expenses during the relocation process, don't expect to include every one of them on the "Moving Expense" form. You may be entitled to a deduction in a different category of your tax return. Keep all of your receipts and consult with a competent tax advisor for more complete information. Only the very basic facts have been outlined in this section.

SECTION 10
COUNTDOWN TO MOVING DAY

"First I was overwhelmed, then depressed, then angry, then organized."
- Connie, a disgruntled housewife who had all of the planning "placed on her lap" after her husband already started his new job 2000 miles away.

The following information will help to minimize last minute headaches and upset stomachs. Many people find themselves running around like a "chicken with its head cut off". While anxiety and nervousness are unavoidable, their levels can be greatly reduced. An organized plan which includes a timetable is extremely important. *It is the only way to reduce most of the last minute chaos.*

Since all of the details outlined will not apply to your set of circumstances, check off the information that does. If necessary, make additional notations in the margin area. (A yellow felt-tip marker can also be used.) As you accomplish each task, cross it out. Constantly refer back to this timetable throughout the entire process.

SIX TO EIGHT WEEKS BEFORE:

Start the "weeding out" process. Have each family member start eliminating unneeded, unwanted, and unused items.

- Sell or give away flammable items.
- Conduct a garage sale.

145

- Decide what you want professionally packed into boxes.

- Obtain estimates from at least 3 moving companies. Review all details and keep asking questions.

- Give written notification to landlord explaining your intention to vacate. (This may need to be done sooner than 6 weeks before leaving, or possibly later in the process.) Whatever your situation may be, giving "proper notification" is essential. Don't overlook this step.

- Arrange to have school records transferred. Obtain copies of college transcripts.

- Use a video camera to inventory contents of each room. Take close-up pictures of antiques and other valuables.

- Accumulate important and/or valuable documents that will be traveling with you.

- Obtain estimates for transporting boxes using alternate methods.

- Obtain prices for travel plans (hotel, airlines, etc.). The Internet can be terrific with this.

- Start collecting a variety of sturdy boxes and newspaper.

- Discuss the transfer of your homeowner's policy and other insurance needs with your insurance agent. If you are transporting "valuables", find out how to get the proper coverage for them.

- Try to obtain a floor plan and room measurements of the new residence.

- Notify all professional people of your intention to relocate (doctor, dentist, pharmacist, banker, veterinarian, lawyer, stockbroker, etc.). Make sure all records are complete and ready to be sent upon request. Ask each one for referrals in your new community.

- Notify banking institutions. Find out what needs to be done when transferring funds to a bank in another state. Establish an account with a bank in the new community. Otherwise, you may have a problem trying to cash checks from an out-of-state account.

- Close local charge accounts with community businesses. However, retain major credit cards until you have an opportunity to obtain new ones through local banks at destination.

- Obtain information about your destination city on the Internet or through the Chamber of Commerce, real estate agent, etc.

- Deliver rugs to the dry cleaners.

- Discuss the upcoming relocation with all family members (especially children). Make each member a part of the planning process. Surprises will only contribute to a traumatic experience. Explain all of the advantages.

- Return borrowed items and collect things loaned to others.

- If your employer is paying for the move, find out exactly what they will pay for. Don't leave anything in doubt.

- If you still need to sell your house, escalate your efforts. If you are working with a real estate company, make sure it is properly advertising the property.

- If you are planning a house-hunting trip, start making arrangements. Try to obtain the Sunday edition of the local newspaper at destination. It will have a large real estate section to guide you. (Once you find a new residence, measure openings for placement of all appliances.)

- Obtain change-of-address cards from the Post Office, and compile a list of those who need to receive one. (Once you have secured a new residence, notify the P.O. and send out cards.) Ask for the "Mover's Guide" at the Post Office. It contains other helpful information.

- Start consuming frozen foods and canned goods.

- If antiques, valuable items and/or collectibles need to be moved, consider obtaining an expert appraisal of each item. In addition, take pictures for verification.

- Obtain IRS "Moving Expense" form. (Your local library or P.O. may have one in stock.) Also, you can get this from the Internet. (www.IRS.gov)

- Do repair work and painting.

FOUR WEEKS BEFORE:

- Select the moving company which offers the best services, at the most reasonable price (even if an exact schedule for loading/delivery is not known yet).
- Begin packing items that are seldom used.
- If your shipment needs to be placed in a self-storage facility at destination, start working on a location through friends, relatives, fellow workers, etc.
- If pets need to be transported, make special arrangements. Get immunization shots and documentation papers from the veterinarian.
- If you are applying for membership to new clubs, apply now if you anticipate a waiting list.
- Inform Federal and State tax agencies, and the State Motor Vehicle Dept. of necessary changes.

TWO WEEKS BEFORE:

- Confirm all travel arrangements.
- If traveling by automobile, have it serviced and totally prepared for the trip.
- If elevator usage is needed, reserve it through the apartment manager.
- Arrange to have grandfather clock/pool table disassembled by an expert. Call the store where they were purchased to get recommendations.
- Notify all utility companies of the exact shut-off date at origin, and the turn-on date at destination (telephone, gas, electric, water).
- Notify other service companies (newspaper, gardener, diaper service, etc.).

- Increase efforts to collect and/or purchase boxes and continue the packing process.

- Ask your employer/manager for a generalized "letter of recommendation". Even though it may not be needed immediately, it's nice to have a year or two later.

- Mail all remaining change-of- address cards. (This is assuming you have a new address at this time.)

- Make sure all tax assessments are paid.

- Call the representative from the moving company selected, to review details and confirm scheduling. If you have added or deleted items, let the representative know. If you want to add extra services or delete a service already added into the total cost, now is the time to update changes. It may be necessary to complete an "addendum" reflecting these changes.

- Start "bidding farewell" to friends and relatives. Make a few phone calls each day. Otherwise, you will be bombarded with calls and personal visits during your last few days. Trying to accomplish last-minute chores will become impossible.

- Call friends, neighbors, and relatives to pick up items you intend to give away.

- Conduct a second garage sale, if the first one was not as successful as you had anticipated.

- Call a charitable organization to make a contribution. (Keep receipt for a possible federal tax deduction.)

ONE WEEK BEFORE:

- Make sure the moving company has all the information necessary to communicate and deliver your shipment (address, telephone number at new residence, at new place of employment, at hotels, motels, at neighbors, friends, relatives, etc.).

- If traveling by car, pack the emergency tool box in the trunk.

- Begin packing all suitcases.

- Pack the "Car-Box", the "Quick-Fix Box", and the "Keep With You At All Times Suitcase".

- Dispose of remaining flammables, aerosol cans, explosives, matches, etc.

- Accumulate all documents/important papers and valuables that are traveling with you.

- Make final arrangements to close and/or transfer bank accounts and safety deposit box. Buy travelers checks and obtain a cashier's check or certified check to pay the moving company.

- Drain fuel and oil from lawn mower, other motorized equipment, and power tools.

- Clean outdoor barbeque. Pack removable parts. (Make sure propane tank is empty.)

- Replace fixtures that will be going and finish minor repair work.

- If your employer is being billed by the moving company, make sure the "purchase order" or "letter of authority" has been received. Since the moving company will conduct a credit investigation, make sure your employer has received credit approval. This is very important! If it has not received something in writing from your company, and approved the company's credit, you will be expected to pay the driver when he arrives at the new residence.

- Arrange to have all major appliances serviced and prepared for the trip. (If you are disconnecting gas/water hook-ups, you can wait until a few days before moving.)

- Arrange for a baby-sitter on "pack-day" and/or moving day.

- If you are shipping boxes through the Post Office or using another alternative, make arrangements to deliver the boxes. Arrange the drop-off in conjunction with your travel plans. You may not want them to arrive too soon.

- If you are entitled to refunds and/or deposit money from utility companies, landlord, or club memberships, make sure they all have your new address. If possible, try to obtain your money while still living there. It beats long-distance telephone calls and letter writing.

- If any legal matters are unresolved, call your attorney to discuss details.

- Start packing pictures, paintings, mirrors, and other wall decorations.

- Sell, donate, or give away remaining house plants.

- Consume food items that are not going with you. Sell or give away what remains.

- Complete all laundry chores.

- Have a "farewell party" for neighbors, friends, and relatives. Keep it simple, and consider using an abundance of paper and plastic products.

- Remove breakables, bottles and jewelry from all drawers. Fill spaces with towels, etc.

ONE-TWO DAYS BEFORE:

- If you are doing your own packing, everything should be ready (except for a few boxes of necessities that can be done on moving day, before the truck arrives).

- Have professional packers arrive to pack the items agreed upon beforehand. (If only a few boxes need to be packed, they are usually done on moving day.)

- Discard items in drawers and cupboards that are not going.

- If residence will be vacant, notify police and neighbors.

- Check steam iron to make sure all water has been drained.

- If you will be paying according to the "actual weight" of your load and have informed the company of your intent to "witness the weighing procedure", call the company to remind them.

- Call and remind baby sitter of schedule. Arrange to have pets out of the way.

- Finish labeling items and/or boxes that state "Do Not Load", "Load Last", "Fragile", "This Side Up", etc.

- Start the cleaning process.

- Prepare a local map for the driver to use to find your new residence.
- Retrieve clothing/rugs from the dry cleaners.
- Disassemble large furniture pieces.
- Confirm airline and hotel/motel reservations.
- Begin packing the car.
- Remind all utility companies, newspaper, and other service companies of shut-off day.
- Put your new address on a small piece of paper and tape it to the side of a kitchen cupboard. The new occupants will need to forward mail that is inadvertently sent to the old address.
- Empty and disconnect major appliances (stove, refrigerator, washer, dryer, window air conditioner, etc.). Plan on going out to dinner on the night before moving day and also on moving day. (Have you collected all appliance manuals for the new owners?)
- Empty, defrost, and clean the refrigerator/freezer and allow to thoroughly dry. Keep checking the drainage tray under the appliance and remove the water. Place baking soda in each compartment.
- Arrange taxi service to the airport. (If you are going in a friend's vehicle, confirm the schedule to arrive in ample time.)

MOVING DAY:

- Finish packing the car.
- Isolate all boxes and suitcases that are traveling with you.
- Stay calm and let the movers do their job. Be available to answer questions.
- Review all details on the "Bill of Lading". Make sure everything, especially the "valuation coverage", is filled in correctly before signing.
- Review all details for delivery. Verify addresses, phone numbers,

scheduling, etc. Provide the driver with a cellular phone number, e-mail address, or new work number.

- Accompany the movers when the inventory is taken. Check their notations and make your own, if necessary. Make sure everything receives an inventory number. Then, sign all inventory sheets and retain a copy.

- Place soft drinks, cold cuts, etc. in a cooler that can be used during the day.

- Remove pillows and blankets from beds. (Leave the mattress/boxspring covers intact.)

- Place trash bags at the curb. If your trash day is not until a few days later, ask neighbors about using their trash cans. It's better than having dogs rip open plastic bags, spreading the contents throughout the neighborhood.

- Vacuum and/or sweep room as it is emptied.

- Check all drawers/closets for remaining items that could have been overlooked. (Have you emptied your secret hiding places?)

- Return keys to new owners, apartment manager, realtor, lawyer, etc.

- Do not use your television sets. Experts say that they should be at room temperature when taken out of a residence. (If they are too hot, cracking may occur.)

- If you notice any damage caused by the movers, make notations on your copy of the inventory and the driver's copy.

- Have cash available to provide a tip for the movers.

- Check all windows and doors to be sure they are locked.

AT DESTINATION:

- Contact the local agent for the moving company to inform the agent of any change in delivery address or telephone numbers.

- Inform the local Post Office of which day you actually plan on moving in. (See if any mail has already been forwarded.)

153

- Arrange to have all utilities turned on. Find out about deposits needed.
- Check plumbing/heating system, electrical outlets, built-in appliances, smoke detectors, etc.
- Do minor repair work, painting and wallpapering. (It is easier when rooms are still empty.)
- Clean entire house. Line cupboards with shelving paper.
- Introduce yourself to neighbors and ask about local stores to buy food, hardware, and other services.
- Have duplicate keys made immediately.
- Arrange for newspaper delivery.
- Register children in the new school system.
- Contact local banks and establish new accounts.
- Contact insurance agent for your immediate needs. (home, automobile, health)
- Contact Department of Motor Vehicles, Voter Registration, and the pet licensing authority.
- Make arrangements to have major appliances reconnected if you are not doing it yourself.
- Check the placement of telephone outlets and arrange to lease or buy new phones, if needed.
- Make arrangements with a long-distance telephone service company. (Shop around!!) You will probably have an immediate need for long-distance communication.
- Contact the local cable company to start service, especially since you will probably have an immediate need to use the Internet!
- Decide on the proper placement of furniture. Discuss which child gets the larger bedroom.
- Tape a small sign on each door that corresponds to labels on cartons. This will allow the movers to quickly place cartons in the proper rooms without you being present.

MOVE-IN DAY:

- Pay the driver, unless other arrangements have been prearranged.

- Check-off numbers on inventory sheets. One person should be outdoors, while a second person is indoors, directing the movers to the proper room locations. Inspect furniture and boxes for possible damage. If any damage is observed or a box is crushed and/or dented, make notations on your copy and the driver's copy of the inventory sheet. Open boxes that appear damaged to inspect the contents while the driver is still there to observe any damage.

- Allow all appliances and televisions a chance to warm up to room temperature before using. This is very important if the outdoor temperature is extremely cold.

- If a battery-operated radio is available, tune into a station that plays relaxing music.

- If you are paying to have the movers do some of the unpacking, supervise this procedure after everything has been positioned in its proper place.

- Do not get involved in trying to unpack everything yourself during the unloading. This can be done in the days that follow.

- Have cash available to tip the movers.

- Arrange to have dinner at a nice restaurant. (Reward yourselves!)

SECTION 11
HELPFUL ORGANIZATIONAL TIPS

"Do not be afraid to ask questions of each moving company. You may get answers that will help you avoid hassles, save time, and maybe even save money".
    -John and Jenny

---

1. When is a good time to begin the packing process?

Start packing infrequently used items, *one month in advance.* Slowly whittle away at this time-consuming chore, a few boxes at a time. Don't underestimate the amount of boxes needed to pack. When purchasing or collecting boxes, make sure you have an ample supply of various sizes. It's better to have a few left over, than to frantically dash around at the last minute when your time is limited.

2. Does it make any difference if I pack similar items from various rooms, in the same box?

Try to pack room-by-room. It will save a bundle of time when unpacking takes place.

3. What can be done to minimize the likelihood of a box getting crushed?

Always place wadded-up paper slightly above the top of a box. Then, apply a little pressure before taping the flaps down. Apply tape to the middle seam, and to both edges. Since some of the boxes may be placed on their side, you don't want the contents to be able to move if that should happen. In theory, pretend you are sitting on a suitcase to squeeze it shut! But, never overpack a box so that it has bulges.

4. Is there anything different about the packing paper used by the professionals, and regular newspaper?

The consistency is about the same. The main difference is that packing paper has no news on it (ink). Never let newspaper come in direct contact with items that can be soiled by the ink. It is fine to use, but you must take a few precautions. First, use tissue paper or plastic baggies, then wrap in newspaper. In addition, constantly wash your hands to remove the ink.

5. Are there any weight limitations for a box?

Never pack boxes so they get too heavy. Keep each box under 50 pounds, since packing tape will only hold so much weight. The last thing you want to see is the bottom falling out of a box.

6. What items should go into a box first?

Place the heaviest things at the bottom. Save the upper area for the lighter and more delicate items.

7. Can pots and pans, silverware and other kitchen items be placed into the same boxes with kitchen dishes, glasses, etc.?

Never pack fragile items in the same box with other categories. Keep them separated to avoid potential damage.

8. Why is it necessary to make notations on the side of a box?

Once boxes are stacked on top of each other, you can't read the notes written on the top. Plus, when everything is unloaded at destination, boxes may be stacked in a room or garage area. They can be easily organized to avoid sore back muscles as a result of moving them around in order to read the notes written on the top.

9. What about packing the prized moosehead and the antique crystal chandelier?

For large, delicate, or odd-shaped items, a wooden crate should be specially constructed. If it's worth moving, it's worth packing properly.

10. Do small furniture items have to be packed into boxes?

If something will conveniently fit in a box, put it in one. Take the time to disassemble little tables, floor lamps, etc. Small foot stools and plant stands should go into boxes. The more uniformity your shipment has, the tighter everything will pack inside the truck. That means less chance for movement and/or shifting of the shipment.

11. Can I pack my small kitchen appliances in the same boxes they came in?

If the original box and packing material is available, use it. Then, consolidate by placing these small boxes into larger sturdy containers.

12. What should I do with the empty boxes once the move is completed?

After unpacking, remove tape so the boxes can be easily folded and stored in a flat position. Place in a dry area of the attic or garage. Usually the open area of the cross-beams near the ceiling is ideal. Place plastic over them to keep clean for the next time. Don't be foolish enough to think there will not be a next time. "Never say, Never!" Plus, you may have a neighbor, family member, or friend that may like to save a few hundred dollars on their next move.

13. Should a protective coating of wax be put on wooden furniture just before loading on the truck?

This makes the furniture slippery and hard to handle. It also increases the likelihood of the furniture pads slipping off due to road vibrations. Once you are settled in, polish everything.

14. How long should I wait before hanging pictures, paintings and mirrors on the walls?

It can take several weeks before you feel totally comfortable with the positioning of furniture in every room. Wait a few weeks before pounding nails into the walls. Unless there is absolutely no other wall where a particular item would look good, restrain yourself for awhile. Resist the immediate temptation to get "hammer happy".

15. Who should be notified that I'm moving? And, what is the easiest way to do it?

Free change-of-address cards can be picked up at any branch of the U.S. Post office. Get a bunch of extras. You'll be surprised how many you'll need! Here is a partial list of whom to notify:

- Local Post Office
- Friends/relatives
- Magazine subscriptions
- Banks
- Credit card companies
- Lawyer
- Doctor/dentist/veterinarian/pharmacist
- Social Security Office/Internal Revenue Service
- Church/synagogue
- Former employer (to send tax form for wages earned)
- Department of Motor Vehicles

Do not forget to stop by the local Post Office at destination immediately upon arrival. There may be mail waiting for you.

16. What needs to be checked on an automobile just prior to a long-distance trip?

Have your mechanic check the brakes and tires. If you are traveling during the winter months, snow tires should be a definite consideration. At the very least, a set of tire chains should be available. The antifreeze and coolant system need to be inspected. In general, a tune-up with a complete inspection ought to be performed. The last thing you need is to be stranded in "no man's land" for a few days!

17. Is there a convenient way to make hotel/motel reservations along the route we intend to be driving?

The Internet can be very helpful with this chore. Also, visit the local branch of a large motel chain to obtain information regarding its national network. Many provide a directory which explains the services offered, prices, and locations. Most will accept major charge cards which provide an easy method of documenting your moving expenses.

18. Since we will arrive at destination before the truck, how can we cut down on motel expenses?

If you don't mind "roughing it" for a few days, consider the use of sleeping bags and air mattresses. These purchases should be cheaper than lodging costs. In addition, instead of receiving a handshake at check-out time, you will still have these items for future use.

19. If we are able to occupy our present residence until the last day of the month, should we schedule the pickup on that day?

Whenever possible, try to schedule the pickup for a few days prior to the date you must legally be out of the residence. This allows some flexibility in case the truck is delayed. Sometimes the driver can be late due to circumstances that are beyond his control (bad weather, mechanical problems, etc.). You don't want the new occupants moving in on the day you are moving out. Try to avoid this potentially hostile encounter!

20. Will the movers remove items in the rafters of a garage/attic, or in a "crawl-space"?

Only if they feel it is safe, and only if they get paid an extra hourly labor charge to do so. They are not obligated to climb ladders; walk across dangerous flooring; go into areas where they cannot stand erect; or go into any area that is not adequately lighted.

21. In this deregulated industry, how can I find out exactly the services, rules and regulations of each company?

In this ever-changing deregulated industry, new programs and services are constantly being introduced. In addition, some may be changed, modified, or eliminated by the time your move actually takes place. Due to extreme competition, many companies are getting creative. A "trial and error" approach has produced some winners, as well as a few losers. It is important to ask each company for details that will confirm all of the information provided.

22. How can I be sure the quality of service will be excellent if companies are discounting?

Only the creative companies that continue to provide the best service, and adjust their philosophy, will survive and flourish. So far, the quality of service provided by the major companies has remained constant, regardless of discounts. While companies may be receiving less revenue for each move, they should be transporting more volume. With a lower price, the gap between using a professional company and a do-it-yourself move is smaller.

23. If my employer is paying for the move, *and has a separate contract with the moving company*, are the same set of rules, regulations, and prices applied?

While interstate moving companies must comply with all D.O.T. requirements, a contract between the moving company and your employer may contain certain conditions or limitations that are perfectly acceptable. This is especially true with government/ military relocations. You should ask your employer and the representative from the moving company about any provisions, exceptions, conditions, or limitations contained in a separate contractual agreement between them.

24. What type of items should I instruct the driver to load last on the van?

It is your responsibility to inform the movers of any items or boxes that you would like to be loaded last. In doing so, they will be the very first things to be unloaded at destination. Typical items would include the vacuum cleaner, rugs and pads, a few boxes containing kitchen supplies or toys for the children.

25. Should I be present when my shipment is weighed?

If you received a non-binding estimate based on the actual weight of your household, it is a good idea to be present *at both weigh-ins*. The truck will drive over a certified scale before arriving on moving day. After the entire shipment is loaded, the driver will return to a scale for a second weigh-in. You will be obligated to pay for the weight difference between those two figures. You have the right to witness both procedures. However, you must inform the company before moving day, so it can properly notify you of the time and place to meet. If you decide to witness the weigh-ins, make sure you are present *both times*.

26. What are common misconceptions concerning free services provided by a professional mover?

Some people expect the movers to disconnect lighting fixtures and appliances, and reconnect everything at destination. Also, some people are shocked to discover that boxes and packing materials are not free.

27. What needs to be done inside the new residence, before the truck arrives?

Scour the entire house using an ample supply of "elbow grease". If you do not know where to purchase some, you are in big trouble! All shelves can be lined with paper if time permits. Start the painting and wallpapering process in the rooms which will contain the most furniture. It will be easier and faster to complete while they are empty. Also, discuss the proper placement for large pieces of furniture; make arrangements with all utility companies; arrange for appliance hookups, if needed; and inspect plumbing/heating systems.

28. How do I obtain information about my new location?

If you are moving to an unfamiliar area, it is a good idea to educate yourself beforehand. Try to get as much information as possible from friends, realtors and others who may be familiar with your new environment. A letter to the Chamber of Commerce or tourist bureau in the area can often be helpful. Also, the Internet can be useful.

Some of the moving companies provide free information about major cities throughout the country. Be sure to ask each representative about this!

Many of the larger real estate companies have an in-house relocation department that provides free literature. They are often affiliated with a separate relocation company. Read through the real estate section in your Sunday newspaper. You should be able to find a few advertisements which say something like – "Relocating? Call our office for free literature about your destination city!" The advertisement will either have a local telephone number to call or a toll-free number. As long as it is free, helpful information, why not education yourself?

SECTION 12
THE DO-IT-YOURSELF INTERSTATE MOVE

"Daddy, is it worth it? I'd be willing to go without candy and gum for a whole year."
- Phillip, Jr., 4 years old, to parents Phil and Elaine, in need of a restroom after the first five miles.

Interstate truck rental companies have continued to increase their rates over the years. Even though interstate movers have also raised their rates, discounting brings them closer to what they were charging 20 years ago. This is good news for the consumer, but not welcomed news for the professional moving companies.

The most common reason for not using a professional company is cost. Those who undertake the "adventure" of a self-move are usually trying to save money. If you are among the young and/ or adventurous-at-heart who are contemplating a do-it-yourself relocation, the following information can be used to estimate the costs involved. When you finish adding up all of the little "extras", you may decide that the money saved is simply not worth the hassle. Do not "bury your head in the sand" while underestimating the total cost. Being unrealistic will only result in financial problems "down the road".

Since your relocation will probably be many miles away, it is doubtful that borrowing a friend's truck will be a possibility. Therefore, you will need to start shopping at truck rental locations to find the best price for a van and any other necessary equipment. Since these companies are as competitive as the professional moving companies, expect the rental rates to vary. In addition, you can expect a variance depending on the size of the truck, the season (higher during the summer months), and the city of origin and destination.

Visit a few of the major truck rental companies in your area. They provide free booklets which explain the equipment available. In addition, the brochures offer advice on how to anticipate what you will need to accomplish this task. (Estimating the proper truck size, packing and loading tips, etc.)

It is extremely important to obtain an accurate estimate for the proper-sized truck. It is common for non-professionals to underestimate the amount of space needed to accommodate a shipment of household goods. There is always "wasted space" due to odd-shaped pieces of furniture. The professional movers are experts at making "every inch count". It is doubtful that you could fit as much into the same amount of space.

The booklets offered by truck rental companies can be helpful in estimating "cubic capacity". In addition, when the representatives from professional moving companies tour your home, they will estimate the total cubic footage needed on their trucks. Since you do not want to leave a bedroom set on the front lawn, get the rental price for a truck that can hold a larger capacity. It's better to be safe, than sorry!

Before you obtain truck rental estimates, a major consideration must be explained. Some of the smaller-sized trucks can be rented with automatic transmissions (11-15 foot vans). A 15 foot truck is only capable of transporting approximately 3 average rooms full of household goods. If you have that many rooms, along with some major appliances or an abundance of items in a garage, attic or basement, there is a good chance you will need a larger-sized truck. If this is the case, you and your traveling companion should be prepared to drive a "stick- shift"! While some companies do have a few of the larger-sized vans equipped with automatic transmissions, they are not readily available.

Use the following outline to arrive at a realistic price.

"I didn't say it would be *easier*, Sweet-cheeks!"

Compare this total estimated cost with those from the professional companies. Then, read the important considerations which follow. Whatever your ultimate decision may be, make it an educated one!

Truck Rental. . . . . ._____

Redistribution Fee. . . . . ._____

Handcart (with and/or without straps). . . . . ._____

Dolly (platform on four wheels). . . . . ._____

Insurance Coverage (for truck damage/accident liability, etc.) _____

Furniture Pads @ $_____ per doz. for _____ dozen = _____

Straps/Ropes (to secure shipment inside the truck). . . . ._____

Boxes and Materials. . . . . ._____

Tolls/Bridges (higher for trucks). . . . . ._____

Permits. . . . . ._____

Tow Bar Rental (for car). . . . . ._____

Loading Labor (friends?). . . . . ._____

State Sales Tax (find out what will be taxed). . . . . ._____

Sub-Total _____

Once you arrive at a sub-total that realistically estimates the cost of all "extras" needed, the cost to purchase gasoline is next. Most rental trucks will get approximately 5-7 miles to a gallon.

Total Miles _____ ÷ 5 miles per gallon = _____ gallons

_____ gallons X $_____ for each gallon = $_____ Total

(When calculating the cost of each gallon, figure high since the main highways will not have cheap "self-service" gas stations for your convenience.)

Add the total estimated cost for gasoline to the sub-total. Now, you are ready to estimate the additional cost for motels and food. When estimating motel costs, be realistic about prices you can expect along the main highways. These rooms are not cheap. In addition, if you need more than one bed, be expecting to pay a higher rate.

Motel cost per night $_____ X _____ nights = $ _____ Total

Food cost per meal $_____ X _____ meals per day = $_____ Total

$ _____ per person X _____ people = $ _____ Total per day

$ _____ total per day X _____ days = $ _____ Total food cost

(When calculating motel and food, you should take into account any extra time needed on the road, since it may take longer than by automobile.)

SUB-TOTAL $ _____

GASOLINE $ _____

MOTEL $ _____

FOOD $ _____

TOTAL ESTIMATED COST $ _____

IMPORTANT CONSIDERATIONS

Now that you realize the amount of money needed to perform the move yourself, compare this price to that of the professionals. If you plan on driving your automobile, you may want to make adjustments to account for expenses that you will have anyway (motel, food, and gasoline for car).

The convenience and safety offered by the professionals is often worth the extra amount. But before making a decision based strictly on dollars and cents, give some thought to a few other important considerations.

Are you and others who will be helping with loading and unloading, physically able to lift the heavy items without risking injury? Back and arm muscles which are not regularly used, will certainly be needed.

- Do you have dependable people at both origin and destination who can definitely be relied upon to show up?

- If you need to hire a person to assist at either end, did you calculate that cost into your total estimate?

- Did you estimate the correct number of furniture pads that need to be rented? Since these are about one-half the size of those used by professionals, you will need to rent almost twice as many. Most items (excluding boxes) will require at least one pad. Therefore, include enough in your estimate. You do not want to be skimpy with padding. This protection will help reduce the likelihood of seeing nicks, scratches and wood chips when unloading.

- What kind of insurance can be purchased in case an accident should occur? Is liability coverage available for injuries, as well as damage to the truck and/or contents?

- What kind of deposit is required on the vehicle? Most companies require a credit card or a large cash deposit.

- Does the rental company guarantee that you will get the truck you need, on the exact day you need it? Will it be the right size, and have all the features you were promised (automatic transmission, radio, air conditioning)? If the company will not provide a written guarantee stating that the truck requested will be available on the day needed, be prepared for the possibility of a delayed departure. While this is not an everyday occurrence, it does happen!

- If you have mechanical problems, who do you contact for repairs or replacement of the truck?

- If the truck breaks down on a highway during the evening hours, what can you do when stranded? If this does happen, will the rental company pay for motel/food expenses, in addition to all necessary repair bills? Will you be expected to pay all of these bills "out of your own pocket", then wait to be reimbursed in the future? Will the company pay the labor cost for reloading the shipment on another truck, if this becomes necessary?

- What is the additional cost for each day you must keep the truck, past the total number of days allowed for your trip? This is especially important for those who must secure a residence at destination. One may not be readily available. Sometimes, you are required to wait until the first day of the following month.

- If your belongings need to be placed in a storage facility at destination, how much will it cost to continue renting the furniture pads? You will still need protection for some of the items being placed on top of each other while being stored.

SECTION 13
MOVING WITHIN THE SAME STATE

Within most states, the moving industry is regulated and monitored by a separate governmental division. It is most often called the Department of Transportation. In some states, the Public Utilities Commission serves as the regulatory agency.

Due to different state regulations, certain provisions in your state may vary from the general explanations in this section. Since each state establishes its own laws, it would not be practical to reproduce all of that information. The result would be a boring encyclopedia of technical jargon.

The important point to remember is that your state has a regulatory/licensing body which monitors the activities of the moving companies it provides with a license. If you are considering the use of a moving company which is not licensed and insured, you are asking for trouble. Simply stated, don't do it!

Most state agencies or Moving and Storage Associations produce and distribute free booklets which clearly outline their basic rules and regulations. Some states even make it mandatory for companies to supply copies of these booklets each time a consumer is provided with a written estimate of cost.

Before you start to entertain bids from various movers, call a local company to ask if it would be kind enough to send you a copy of your state's booklet. It will probably be happy to do so, since the company will be assuming you will call back when it is time to do business. After receiving the booklet, read it very carefully. It will outline your responsibilities and obligations to a moving company, as well as the company's obligations to you.

Whether you are moving around the comer, across the state, or across the country, proper planning is the key to a successful and positive experience. It can be exciting, or it can be a big hassle for you and your entire family.

Hopefully, you can start the process a few months in advance. To give you a good idea of where to begin, read Section 10 (Countdown To Moving Day). Use a pencil to circle or check off each detail that pertains to your set of circumstances.

Throughout this section, it will be necessary for you to constantly refer back to previous pages. While this interrupts the natural flow of your reading, it is necessary to isolate this information. Otherwise, combining different sets of rules and regulations for various types of relocations into the same discussion would only result in confusion.

Since other sections were written to help those moving in a deregulated environment, from one state into another (interstate move), you will need to filter out information that is unrelated to your move within the same state (local or intrastate move). For instance, many states do not allow any form of guaranteed price estimates or discounting of prices for moves within state boundaries. If this is the case in your state, disregard references to Binding, "Not To Exceed", Guaranteed, "Bottom Line" discounts, etc.

Once you finish reading this book, you will certainly have some questions. Write them down as they surface. When the sales representatives are in your home to explain their services and to provide an estimate of cost, ask them to address your questions and concerns. Lastly, ask them to clarify any state rules, regulations, laws, or company policies and procedures which differ from interstate regulations.

When contacting an office to make an appointment for a sales representative to visit your home, ask if there is any charge for providing a written estimate of cost. Some states allow moving companies to charge a small fee, while others do not even require that one be given. Find out what is going on in your community. Ask to personally speak with the representative on the telephone before making an appointment. Filter out the ones that are less helpful and unwilling to take the time to briefly answer your preliminary questions. Give priority treatment to the ones who are willing to provide a free written estimate of costs. Avoid oral agreements, if at all possible!

HOW TO SELECT A MOVER

When you are ready to begin shopping for the "right" moving company, read about what "Mr. Smart" does (Section 3) for interstate moves. However, remember that many states forbid Binding/Guaranteed Estimates and discounting on moves within their boundaries. A consumer's ability to negotiate in a regulated atmosphere will be less flexible, and often prohibited by state law.

In order to protect consumers from gross miscalculations and mistakes made by a moving company's sales representative, many states have adopted some sort of consumer protection policy. The most common protection against underestimating the total cost has been similarly patterned after the "estimate, plus 10% rule" (Read Section 1 for an explanation).

The good news is that some of those states also feel that you should not have to pay a dime more than the itemized written "estimate, plus 10%" . This is the next best thing to receiving a guaranteed total price for all services listed on a written estimate. Therefore, always try to get everything in writing, and ask each sales representative for a thorough explanation of existing consumer price protection laws within your state.

HOW PAYMENT IS MADE

For local or long distance moves within state boundaries, the method of payment, most often, will be determined by a particular company's own policy, not by state law. One company may allow payment by personal check or credit card, while another might insist on payment in cash, certified check, travelers checks, money order, etc. Ask each company about its policy well in advance.

MOVING LOCALLY (HOURLY LABOR COST)

In many communities, the minimum hourly rate charged by a licensed household mover is established by the state. Many states have a "Minimum Rate Tariff" which not only explains rules and regulations, but also establishes the minimum amount that licensed movers must charge for certain services in their state. If these restrictions exist in your community, movers may be allowed to charge more than the minimum amount, but never less.

Friendly competition within your community will usually be a major factor in determining the hourly rate you will ultimately have to pay. This will be especially true if your state does not provide pricing restrictions.

Even though your state may not have a minimum amount for the total hours in which the labor will be performed, some moving companies may demand that you pay for a certain amount of total hours, even though the labor is completed in less time. This normally depends on the "supply and demand" principle and, also, on the location of both residences.

For example, if your move needs to be performed at a time when a particular company is extremely busy, it might inform you in advance that you will be charged for at least eight hours of labor, even though the move could possibly be completed in less time.

The location of both residences, as well as the "travel time" between them and the moving company's facility, can sometimes require that you pay for a minimum amount of total hours. It often depends on when "the company's clock starts ticking away, and when it stops ticking". You will have to find out how each company "operates its clock". Will you be paying from the time the truck leaves and returns to the warehouse? Or does the clock start when the movers are at your door, and stop when they complete their work at the new residence? Will any amount of "travel time" be added on? These important questions should be asked of each moving company under consideration. How a company "operates its clock" will either be determined by state law or individual company policy.

176

Whenever possible, try to avoid scheduling your local move on weekends and during the very beginning or end of any month. The availability of trucks and personnel to properly handle the large volume of business during these periods can sometimes present a problem. Most working people want to move on a Saturday so they do not have to take a day off from work. And with rental leases expiring and house closings occurring on the first or last days of each month, a few mechanical problems with the trucks could lead to a disaster for you and the moving company. Also, since the demand is high and the availability of equipment and personnel is low during these periods, companies may be charging more money.

When you are ready to start shopping for a mover, spend a few minutes on the telephone talking to four or five local companies. As a result, you should quickly learn the competitive hourly rate; who may be charging for a total hourly minimum; how "travel time" will be computed, etc. Since one company may be busier than another, it will pay for you to shop around!

MOVING LONG DISTANCE
(COST BASED ON WEIGHT)

If you are moving quite a distance away from your present community, calculating the cost on an hourly basis would not be very practical. Therefore, once the relocation exceeds a "reasonable distance", the transportation charge will be based on total poundage and total mileage (Section 1).

This "reasonable distance" varies in each state. One may be 30 miles, while another might be 50 miles. When your new residence exceeds your state's mileage requirement, the amount of hours it takes to load, drive, and unload at destination will not effect the basic transportation charge. It will simply be based on total weight and mileage. Therefore, think of ways to "lighten the load", just like any other type of move (Section 7).

Depending on the location of your present and future residence; the time of the year; and the availability of a particular company's equipment/manpower, you may discover that "lightening the load" might not make a difference in the transportation cost. Because of these three factors, a company might charge for a *minimum amount of total poundage* even though the actual weight might be lower. When a company is going to do this, it should inform you beforehand.

Upon discovering that you will be paying for 8000 pounds when the sales representative estimated your total weight at 5000 pounds, it would hardly make sense to discard or dump anything. In this situation, why not take everything! But, before agreeing to pay for a minimum amount of total weight, call a few more companies. Some may not require any minimum, or may have a lower minimum amount. Usually this is determined by company policy, not state law. Ideally, you want to pay for the actual weight. Nothing more, and nothing less!

STORAGE

When household goods are to be stored at a local warehouse and delivered out locally, the labor cost is usually calculated on an hourly basis. Then, the monthly storage and "warehouse handling charge" (if any) will usually be figured according to how many wooden vaults/pallets are needed. If a company charges $25 for each vault and the shipment is placed into 4 vaults, the monthly charges will be $100 plus the cost for insurance if you elect to take some out. If a very large item will not fit into a vault (large sofa, rug, piano, etc.), expect to pay a small additional amount for this item to be stored separately.

Some states provide the option of having local storage-related charges based on total poundage. If your state allows both methods of calculating, ask each sales representative to figure the cost both ways. If both methods result in a similar total, using the poundage method is recommended. If the movers happen to work very carefully, but very slowly, you will not have to pay for their extra time when the cost is based on weight.

In addition, you should not have to pay more for the monthly

178

storage charge if your household goods need to be placed into more wooden vaults than the sales representative originally estimated. Of course, if your belongings weigh more than originally estimated, all storage related costs will be more, respectively.

When presented with both pricing alternatives, making the proper choice can often be confusing. As you are obtaining three or four written estimates, ask each sales representative for recommendations. If you are still confused, get a few more written estimates. You will not only learn more about different pricing options, but you will also gain more confidence in the estimates of total poundage.

If you are ultimately moving out of your present community and the transportation cost is being based on total poundage, the labor charge to pick up or deliver to or from a company's storage facility will most often be calculated by using the same poundage.

The length of time your possessions need to be stored will sometimes determine which method is used to calculate labor charges, as well as other storage costs. A storage period of 90 days or less (this duration varies between states) is commonly called Storage-In-Transit (S.I.T.). This term means that storage is needed in conjunction with a move that is based on weight.

Many states have similarly patterned their S.I.T. rules and regulations after those established for interstate movers. Therefore, if you need a more detailed explanation, review Section 6, and also ask each sales representative for an explanation of how your state's laws and regulations may differ.

THE EXTRAS

When paying by the hour, most time-related extra charges discussed in Section 6 will not be computed separately. If any of the three "special conditions" or extra pickups/deliveries are part of a local move, the additional cost will be reflected in the increased time it takes to complete the move. However, even on hourly moves, most states allow movers to charge for "overtime labor"; for "special handling charges"; and for arranging "third-party services".

If your move is based on total weight, expect to pay for most of the "extras" discussed in Section 6. Even though prices and regulations may differ slightly, most states allow moving companies to charge for these similar circumstances and services. Therefore, if you want to avoid arguments and hassles on moving day, discuss everything with each sales representative. The movers who actually perform the work are often paid on a percentage basis by the moving company. Don't think they do not know what they are entitled to!

THE "BREAK POINT"

If you are being charged according to the actual weight of your household goods, the "breakpoint" principle will also apply to your move within state boundaries. (See Section 4)

ORGANIZING THE UNLOADING PROCESS

When moving locally, procedures at destination are less complicated. Payment is usually easier to arrange, and inventory sheets are normally not used. You simply point the movers in the right direction so they can quickly and safely be on their way home. Less time, less money!

When a long distance move needs to be unloaded, most of the basic procedures as those discussed in Section 5 will need to be followed.

IRS TAX DEDUCTIONS
FOR MOVING EXPENSES

The same rules apply as those pertaining to interstate moves. Moving expenses are deductible on federal income taxes. Also, you must meet the same time test, distance test, and the relocation must be job-related. If you are moving locally, you will have a hard time meeting the distance requirement! (See Section 9)

OBTAINING BOXES

Use the same methods as outlined in Section 7. In addition, ask each moving company if it sells or provides free, used ones. Unlike the regulations for interstate moves, some states allow companies to supply used boxes. Some permit them to be sold at a fraction of the cost. Inquire about this!

PACKING

The same packing procedures should be followed if any box is loaded on a truck. However, if your move is a short distance away and space is available to store items at destination prior to moving day, consider shuttling open boxes back and forth in your car. This will reduce the amount of boxes you must obtain, and unpacking on moving day will go faster.

In most states, packing labor can be performed on an hourly basis, instead of the "per box" basis used on interstate moves. In general, this is good news! The labor cost on a "per box" basis can often multiply out to more money. However, problems can arise when you have a professional packer who works in slow motion. If he or she only packs two boxes per hour, you are in trouble.

Depending on the nature of what needs to be packed, a professional packer should be able to pack 5 boxes per hour. (Fewer if dishes and breakables, more if books, tools, etc.) (See Section 7)

ADDENDUM (MAKING CHANGES)

If any changes need to be made on the original written estimate of cost or order form, a change order (sometimes called an "addendum") can be used. (See Section 4)

BILL OF LADING (CONTRACT)

This is the legal contract between you and the moving company. It should be signed by both parties before the move begins. (See Section 4)

DRIVER'S INVENTORY

While your state may not require the movers to take a comprehensive written inventory, most movers will complete these sheets, especially for poundage moves. On local hourly moves, it is not very common. Besides, when you are paying by the hour, it is unlikely you would voluntarily want to pay for this extra time unless you had no trust in the competence and integrity of the company you selected. (See Section 4)

LIABILITY COVERAGE (INSURANCE)

Every state has its own rules, regulations, and laws regarding insurance and liability coverage. You can obtain this information by reading your state's consumer booklet, and by asking questions of each sales representative. If you have homeowners insurance, place a call to your insurance agent. It may be possible that you already have some form of limited coverage in your existing policy. It won't hurt to ask.

An explanation of liability coverage for interstate moves will provide you with a very general idea of how it works. Keep in mind that your state insurance laws will be different; the rules and methods used to file a claim will be different; and the type of coverage that movers are allowed to provide will also vary from state to state. (See Section 4)

SHIPPING BOOKS AND ALTERNATE METHODS OF SHIPPING BOXES

When moving locally, try to take the majority of the boxes to your new residence by using available automobiles. Leave the larger boxes for the movers to take with the furniture. This will cut down on the amount of hours you must pay for. A lot of time is wasted moving boxes from residence to truck, and again from the truck into the new residence.

When moving long distance, if convenient, take a few of the heavier boxes in the car. If you have a large quantity, consider renting a small trailer that can be safely towed behind your automobile.

Since the rates within your state (dollars and cents for each 100 pounds, moving so many miles) are not as high as those for a move going across country, it is unlikely you will save any money by using other methods of shipping your boxes (Post Office, UPS, etc.). In fact, it will probably cost more than if you had the movers put the boxes on the truck.

THE DO-IT-YOURSELF MOVE

No matter how far you are moving, most of the information in Section 12 will be useful. However, on a local or short-distance relocation, the potential for problems with truck availability greatly diminishes. Also, since you often pay on a "per day" basis for local moves where mileage has no bearing on the rental cost, renting a truck is undoubtedly the cheapest method. If you or your friends and family members have strong backs, and are available to load as well as unload a rented truck, by all means consider this option. However, be certain your helpers are dependable, and be prepared for damage claims that are "uncollectible".

COMMENTS?

The publisher and author are extremely interested in hearing from you. (Both good news and/or bad news!)

This information will enable us to help others in the future, and will be incorporated in the next edition of this book.

Comments (attach separate sheet, if necessary):

Name: _____

Address: _____

City:_____State:_____Zip: _____

Telephone (optional): _____

Please send comments to the address below, and let us know if we have permission to use your comments in the future.

_____Yes, you may use my name when quoting from my comments.

Signature: _____

TRANSPORTATION PUBLISHING CO.
P.O.Box 2309-B
Mission Viejo, CA 92690

Send E-mail to henrymovesme@cox.net

Website: www.yourgoodmove.com

ORDER FORM

Transportation Publishing Co.
P.O. Box 2309-B
Mission Viejo, CA 92690

Please send me _____ copies of <u>Moving? Don't Let a Moving Company Take You For An Expensive Ride</u> at $19.95 each, plus $4.50 to cover shipping/handling costs.
(Add $1.00 for each additional copy)

Name: _____

Address: _____

City:_____State:_____Zip: _____

* For shipments within California add $1.55 sales tax per book.

---

* Would you like to order this book as a special gift for a friend, neighbor or relative anticipating a relocation? Please indicate the complete name and address of person(s) to receive a copy.

Name: _____

Address: _____

City:_____State:_____Zip: _____

Or visit our website: www.yourgoodmove.com

Or send E-mail to: henrymovesme@cox.net

NOTES:

NOTES:

NOTES:

NOTES:

NOTES: